The Healing Imagination

STUDIES IN PASTORAL PSYCHOLOGY, THEOLOGY, AND SPIRITUALITY
Robert J. Wicks, General Editor

also in this series

Clinical Handbook of Pastoral Counseling
edited by R. Wicks, R. Parsons, and D. Capps
Adolescents in Turmoil, Parents Under Stress
by Richard D. Parsons
Pastoral Marital Therapy
by Stephen Treat and Larry Hof
The Art of Clinical Supervision
edited by B. Estadt, J. Compton, and M. Blanchette
The Art of Passingover
by Francis Dorff, O. Praem.
Losses in Later Life
by Scott Sullender
Pastoral Care Emergencies
by David K. Switzer
Spirituality and Personal Maturity
by Joann Wolski Conn
Christointegration
by Bernard J. Tyrrell, S. J.
Adult Children of Alcoholics
by Rachel Callahan, C.S.C. and Rea McDonnell, S.S.N.D.
Health Care Ministry
edited by Helen Hayes, O.S.F. and Cornelius J. van der Poel, C.S.Sp.
Surviving in Ministry
edited by Robert R. Lutz and Bruce T. Taylor

The Healing Imagination

The Meeting of Psyche and Soul

Ann and Barry Ulanov

Integration Books

paulist press / new york / mahwah

* * *

Acknowledgements

We would like to thank Robert Wicks, our editor, for his unobtrusive and persistent support. We are grateful to Rosannah Cole for her skill and graciousness in the typing of our manuscript.

Library of Congress Cataloging-in-Publication Data

Ulanov, Ann Belford.
The healing imagination: the meeting of psyche and soul/Ann and Barry Ulanov.
p. cm.—(Integration books)
Includes bibliographical references.
ISBN 0-8091-3245-1
1. Imagination—Religious aspects—Christianity. I. Ulanov, Barry. II. Title. III. Series.
BR115.I6U43 1991
233—dc20 91-3877
CIP

Published by Paulist Press
997 Macarthur Boulevard
Mahwah, New Jersey 07430

Printed and bound in the
United States of America

Contents

For Nathan and Ralph,
our fathers

Foreword

Images of fabulous originality rise up out of our psyche continuously. How we greet them does not determine their power; they always have power. But it does affect whether this constant force in our lives is a source of positive or negative development.

In their book *The Healing Imagination,* Ann and Barry Ulanov effectively plunge us into this often misunderstood, ignored, and misappropriated area of energy deep within: the area of imagination. In this work they encourage us to "let the images be there," to open ourselves to the primordial truths which images may carry and not to avoid this God-given source of potential knowledge and healing.

As with anything that contains truth, images can deliver a sense of dread as well as possibilities of hope at the same time, in the same space. The Ulanovs encourage us to have respect for, deep interest in, and strong involvement with, the vast archetypal world that our imagination opens up to us. They rightly appreciate that "our refusal to use our imagination costs not only our imagination but reality. For unacknowledged, unreceived fantasies invade reality all the more demandingly and eventually usurp its place."

The Healing Imagination is a clearly-written book on the tapestry and complexity of imagination. In approaching the topic, it draws upon numerous sources and honestly describes how imagination can both harm as well as heal. It argues convincingly that we must appreciate the value within all imagery while avoiding the danger of being simplistic in our interpretation and acquiescence to their apparent messages. In essence, the call that is made in this marvelously descriptive little book is to put aside undue fear and accept what God offers us afresh each day through the psyche in the healing possibilities of our imagination.

Imagination, if we embrace it, offers us the chance to—in the imagery of sacred scriptures—leave the "ninety-nine" (those consciously acceptable parts of ourselves) and to reach out to what appears alien in our relationship with ourselves, others, and God. In other words, imagination is one of the essences of creative solidarity. And in this book the Ulanovs help us to recognize this point.

The Healing Imagination also discusses the essential role played by our sexuality in being open to the vitality of the imaginative process. Rich imagery without sexuality is a bit like trying to describe a colorful gray photograph. One wonders whether it is possible. In addition, special attention is given to the topic: "Who Feeds the Feeder?" This chapter, in particular, offers such a creatively helpful appreciation of why and how one needs to be educated in the ways of the unconscious that even standing alone it makes the Ulanov book an innovative resource for people called to leadership positions in their church. In it the authors show us that with imagination we can travel to the heart of our motivations and sit in this space with God. From there we can see both the challenges and the compulsions of ministerial approaches to helping others with emotional needs and spiritual hunger.

This little volume of ideas and reflections on the subject of imagination is drawn to a close by chapters entitled "Prayer and Politics" and "Resurrection." In these chapters as in the entire book, we are treated not only to an appreciation of the topic of imagination in general, but to the gifts that Barry and Ann Ulanov themselves have as imaginative people. Consequently, in reading *The Healing Imagination,* you not only learn about the subject, but you experience it with them. I found this book to be both enlightening and healing, and for this I thank them professionally . . . and personally.

Robert J. Wicks
Series Editor

Chapter 1

The Healing Imagination

There is no life of the spirit without the imagination. Without it, the psyche stands undefended, undernourished, at less than half strength. And yet people constantly belittle or trivialize it—"You're just imagining that!" "Your imagination is playing tricks again!"—or even doubt they possess it at all. Poets and painters, they think, have imagination, not ordinary people. When its presence is unmistakable, it frightens because of its power to control or to distort. Still it remains what it has always been, a central resource of the life of the psyche and of the life of the spirit. Properly understood and pursued, the imagination is perhaps our most reliable way of bringing the world of the unconscious into some degree of consciousness and our best means of corresponding with the graces offered us in the life of the spirit. It accomplishes these things as it performs its more prosaic task of confirming the reality of the world around us, of people, of objects, not by mere observation, but by its slow, deliberate taking in and filling out. The imagination brings completion.

We take counsel with ourselves in the realm of the imagination. With it, we move toward ends. Images linger. Sounds abide. Even tastes and touches and smells can be experienced again, however uncertainly defined. We see how much of what we do requires construction or reconstruction, invention or reinvention. We think our way back, we feel our way toward what has happened to us in the past that we would like to hold onto and to keep in being through the imagination. We do the same with possible events to come: we fit them out with their identifying shapes and smells, their size, their duration. If they suggest pleasure, we use our imagination to revel in it. If they threaten, we have the resources of an instructed fantasy to help us cope. But we may never get to this point. We may be too fearful about the imagination itself.

The imagination does frighten people. Too many of us think of it as a specialized skill or talent, the gift of the literary imagination, for example, something for which we need expert training as we do to paint or to design a dress. Even those who are specialists, such as people in religion, can be markedly scared of the imagination.[1] It is not exactly in vogue in church, synagogue, or temple. It promises to take us far outside what religion defines as allowed; our imaginings may compete with scripture. Imagination may seem off the ground, then, a rarefied and esoteric activity that is too far separated from daily life tasks and burdens to be taken seriously, too precious for the work most of us have to do, the activity of a dubious elite.

It may be that imagination frightens us because it is something we all possess and exercise, at least some of the time, but are uneasy about naming. That diminishes its effects. That keeps us from its healing touch. We fear to engage it directly, to admit to ourselves what we are really doing. We fear to know what, in fact, we do know. Is it because it reaches so far back into the sources of being? Jung suggests as much: How can this be? What could be so frightening about imagining?

"I am indeed convinced," Jung says, "that creative imagination is the only primordial phenomenon accessible to us, the real Ground of the psyche, the only immediate reality. Therefore I speak of *esse in anima* [Being in the soul], the only form of being that we can experience directly."[2]

For us to imagine, in something like full consciousness, is to be in being, directly, without mediation. When we construct images of a house we would like to have or a room we would like to live in, we are creating structures to house our being. We are picturing how being might be and how we would help shape it to be.[3] The same happens when we imagine how we would like to appear—what look we might have, something all the commercial magazines capitalize on by making us see ourselves as doomed to be dumpy, drab, hopelessly out-of-date until we buy the advertised jackets, coats, shirts, dresses and suits. When we hold images of people we love in our minds—the eyes of a long-time friend, the death of a parent, the fresh complexion of a daughter or son, the body of our beloved, so vivid to us that a scent accompanies the image—we are creating and re-creating the love between us and the others. We add to the love as we celebrate the fact that it exists and has existed. Imagination feeds reality.

When a vivid dream image carries itself into our waking hours—an old crone, an arousing other, the sound of leaves rustling—it imbues the whole day with another presence. Though unseen, that presence adds another line of perception. We carry it around in us like a secret, a magic stone hidden in our mitten. Everything we touch then takes on an added glow of meaning. When we feel haunted by images of our own insufficiency, whether it is a face full of marks or another body-part that bulges instead of lying flat or that lies flat instead of billowing out, or when we feel barren, incompetent, discontinuous, having dropped the thread that strings our parts and experiences together, losing the people and events of our past and much of ourselves as well, then the power of images to crush us makes itself felt. Worse still, dream images can surround us with menacing gestures and atmospheres that follow us through the waking day—insect hordes emerging from a hole in our bed, a viscous mass trapping our feet, or a man pursuing us with an ax or a woman with a knife.

Imagination can terrify, and we do not have to go to sleep to feel besieged by it. Images of evil leap up at us in each day's news. We have reason to fear the plentiful attackers and destroyers of our world. Rape, murder, war have become commonplace events in our time. Earthquake, genocide, paranoic mass killers have become grimly familiar facts in our landscapes of terror. The gentle ironies of poets send them to prison or death in totalitarian countries. Osip Mandelstam, killed in a gulag because of his satirical poem about Stalin, said the USSR was the only state that took poetry seriously. Irina Ratushinskaya, confined to a Soviet security prison, saw recorded on her dossier, *Crime: poet.*[4] We live or die in our images. Totalitarian dictators know that. So does a teacher seeing in them her students' potentialities and working to bring them to life. Another kind of teacher, burdened by the negative images of demanding, harassing students, can cast a pall of death over the classroom.

Imagination is all but palpable. It brings not only new pictures but new sensations. It does not rely on the eye alone. Some people hear sounds in their dreams—the growling of a beast, a word spoken, strains of music. Some people smell in their dreams—the foul odors of backed-up toilets or fetid water, or the sweet ones, of a mother's cologne or of baking bread. Touch figures large in our images, in dreams of velvet or of animal fur or of tactile human exchanges that linger through the day into the night. We feel again a lover's hair on the face, skin, and muscle against our legs. We imagine the frowsy wobbly head of our newborn child nuzzled in the hollow of our neck. We can sense the fragrant thinness of tender spring grass in our nostrils, against our lips. We hear again the thunk of tennis balls, the jumble of radio music, car horns, people chattering, the whoosh of tires on hot asphalt in a summer city street. We can imagine the space around us as we enter prayer, or we can feel our backs constrict and our necks crunch down in abject shame over something we have done, or not done, that we must confess, at least to ourselves. And then all the senses may suddenly rush together in an exuberance of imagination, where things are simultaneously seen, heard, touched, smelled, and tasted. The saints talk about tasting Christ, feeling his presence touch them, seeing a glow, actually hearing him speak.[5]

The miracle of the imagination, and the secret of its healing power, is that it can stretch from the most trivial event to the most profound and not lose its capacity to deal with either extreme. Things are constantly reborn in the imagination, made fresh, brought to us to renew themselves and to renew us. Coleridge, the grand philosopher of the imagination, says that what caught him immediately in the work of his fellow poet Wordsworth was "the union of deep feeling with profound thought; the fine balance of truth in observing, with the imaginative faculty in modifying, the objects observed. . . ." Renewal was the effect. Wordsworth spread "the tone, the atmosphere, and with it the depth and height of the ideal world, around forms, incidents, and situations of which, for the common view, custom had bedimmed all the lustre, had dried up the sparkle and the dewdrops."

The genius of a poet like Wordsworth is, for Coleridge, to "carry on the feelings of childhood into the powers of manhood; to combine the child's sense of wonder and novelty with the appearances which every day for perhaps forty years had rendered familiar. . . ."[6] Is that a power restricted to genius? Undoubtedly the answer is Yes if we are talking about making a poem of Wordsworthian freshness and clarity. But to retain a child's astonishment in the face of things with which we are intimately acquainted is not limited to poetic genius. Aesthetic judgment, as a philosopher who was not a poet, Immanuel Kant, insisted, is each person's own to make, based on each one's own experience. The urgent issue is how far we reach for that experience, how well educated the judgment is, how open we remain to the power of the imagination.

The power is familiar enough. How often we hear, "If you would just stretch your imagination. . . ." When the stretching becomes a necessary part of our setting-up exercises for every day and for every night, we find ourselves at the center of things. That is to say, we find our Selves. With or without a poet's warrant, we accept the possibility of living with our own being, of inspecting it, of seeing all its positive and negative qualities, and of accepting it. With our imagination stretched, we enter the healing precincts where scarred surfaces or pitted insides really are acceptable and so are the accomplishments of body and psyche and soul, whatever their size. All of us are grounded in this immediate reality of being. It is what allows us to be our individual selves, to live with ourselves and others, and what makes it possible for others to live with us. This being-in-ourselves which is also a being-with-others is the reality that the imagination constantly confirms. And so again we ask, Why are we frightened by the imagination? What is it that we do not want to know about it? What is it that we do not think we have experienced or, more seriously, do not think we can ever experience?

What frightens us about the imagination is the power of being right there inside ourselves, and in much the same way, inside each of our neighbors. With such power, any of us at any time, can wound anyone, even fatally, by the imaginative conception we carry of each other.[7] We all know such withering experiences. Someone treats us with contempt, looks down on us as if we were a slug, slimy and detestable. If we have read Gertrud Kolmar, that heroic poet in Nazi-occupied Berlin who persisted in writing poetry in her brief breaks from crushing factory labor, we know the secret life borne in the images of the toad, the snail, the lizard.[8]

But must we reduce others to toads and slugs? Must we treat them—or ourselves—with contempt? Any of us can enlighten others and show another way of perceiving the self that is also in each of us. We can show the person the beauty we hold within us, the hopes we have harbored, the great reach toward Being which we all feel at some time or another, a Being we move toward because it is here, now, for the taking, and somehow we know that it is. Karl Menninger said we fail not in science but in hope, and we would add that we fail as much again in faith.[9]

We lose our faith in human possibility, our imagination shrinks, we dare not hope, and we leave our neighbors languishing in mental hospitals and substandard housing, in stifling cities and classrooms with a pall of death over them. Social projects get ignited from images of their possibility. Gaston Bachelard says of poetry that it is the first articulation of Being. So it is with our shared life: images of betterment initiate the building of vest-pocket parks, gifted architects designing middle-income apartment buildings in West Berlin, captive nations freeing themselves from what seemed an undefeatable tyranny by the sheer force of their collective faith and hope.[10]

What frightens us is the power and closeness of Being, right there inside us and among us. What would happen if all of us took full freedom with our imaginations? It might lead each of us to the divine spark within us, there under the rubble of neglect, all but crushed by the tyranny of the prosaic, lead us to the place where we can create the selves we are meant to be.[11]

Does the imagination hold such force? Can it possibly possess such a capacity, assert such authority in our lives, infuse the neglected sides of our self with so much energy? Coleridge's defining terms for the imagination all say Yes to these questions.

For him, there are in effect two imaginations: "The primary imagination I hold to be the living power and prime agent of all human perception, and as a repetition in the finite mind of the eternal act of creation in the infinite I AM." The essential liberating or creative power of the imagination, which exists in each one of us, is nothing less than a copy of perfect Being, however reduced in scale and translated from the simple seamless majesty of the divine into the complex scattering of parts which is our being. That is what leads Coleridge to the definition of the secondary imagination, a world of process and potentiality, and above all a world vibrant with life:

> The secondary I consider as an echo of the former, coexisting with the conscious will, yet still as identical with the primary in the kind of its agency, and differing only in degree, and in the mode of its operation. It dissolves, diffuses, dissipates, in order to re-create; or where this process is rendered impossible, yet still, at all events, it struggles to idealize and to unify. It is essentially *vital,* even as all objects (as objects) are essentially fixed and dead.

For Coleridge, the principal work of the secondary imagination lies in poetry. There, the echoings and mirrorings of "the eternal act of creation in the infinite I AM" can be translated into finite terms. There, the results of an inspired breaking up and spreading out can be seen, and even if inspiration lags we can at least experience the great effort necessary to bring things together and point to ideal forms if not necessarily realize them. Poets do these things as a mark of their gifts, and especially the precious one of the literary imagination. But the genius of Coleridge in his definition is not to restrict his understanding of the imaginative faculties to poets. The primary imagination is the essential instrument of "all human perception." It moves at some level in all of us. It is the animating force of our sensations.[12]

None of this requires intention or any significant degree of consciousness. In some way, whether we deliberately bring images to mind or not, the imagination is alive in us, stretching, reaching out to what has been called the All of Reality. However little we may be schooled in the interior life, however unwilling we may be to accept the existence of a deeper presence in ourselves, it is there, and the agency of the imagination, primary and secondary both, constantly asserts the fact that it is so. Our subjectivity, our ego-life, by its familiar habits of operation insists on something larger than itself, some indwelling signification of being to which, like it or not, we give assent simply because we are sentient beings, because we can touch, taste, smell, hear, see, and bring to the experience of the senses the corroboration of mind that comes in image and judgment.

The closeness of this reading of the imagination to the understanding of the psyche of Sigmund Freud, and the depth psychology that he set in being, is unmistakable. What he called primary and secondary process are categories more than obliquely related to the primary and secondary imagination of Coleridge. Freud was describing by these terms the unconscious and the strategies of the conscious by which we draw into varying degrees of awareness its currents, its images, its enactments and reenactments, its displacements, its whole astonishing repertoire. Freud would not himself accept the possibility of a sacred presence somehow instinct in unconscious process. The superego that he saw at work in human life was an altogether identifiable set of authorities in society, in the family, in teachers, in the military, in the professions, in the cadres of the law, in the bosses of all kinds with whom we are only too liberally supplied. We need no further sanction to motivate our responses to the world around us. The tug of the unconscious, the fear or love of what we choose to give authority in our lives, our sexuality, our attempt to formulate some sense of a person for ourselves—these are enough.

But are they? Do they reach far enough into the complexity of human performance? Can we forswear the operations of the spirit as comfortably—or uncomfortably—as Freud did? To account for the creative power that the least of us experiences in the activity of the imagination, don't we have to enlarge our reading of human functioning beyond ego and superego, id (the pull of the unconscious) and libido (desire)? Freud accounts for much, and ingeniously, but not for enough. Too much in the psyche and beyond the psyche demands further accounting. How does there come to be something rather than nothing in the mind? Why are so many of us not content to see ourselves in the fourfold reduction of Freud, any more than we can settle into the mazes of behaviorism where everything we do is predetermined and what we think is free choice turns out to be no more than the end-product of a causal series? How do we really know that other people exist, have feelings, think, come to know us? What are the roots of sympathy, not only for our own level of being, but for so many others, reaching beyond the human? How do we find connection with the worlds of animals, of plants and flowers and trees, of rocks and waters? Why do we quicken so at the possibility of love, even a clumsy one, a far from fulfilling one, a degrading one?

Primary and secondary process as categories of the psyche are helpful in dealing with these questions, but the questions go beyond the psyche to the soul. They require more of the imagination than even so gifted an employer of its faculties as Freud was able or willing to yield to it. He thought that his "discovery" of the unconscious was a feat of Copernican dimensions. He would have been wiser, perhaps, to think of it in Coleridgean terms.

It is of more than passing interest that Freud's chosen successors, his "sons" and heirs apparent, decided against him in these matters. First Carl Jung and then Otto Rank insisted on a much larger reading of the psychic field than Freud had given. Their understanding demanded a much more spacious vision. The imagination of the psychoanalyst had to be stretched to include the world of spirit. Jung makes this clear in the eloquent little paper he published in a Cologne newspaper in 1929 on the *Gegensatz*, the essential difference, between his thinking and Freud's. The warning is direct:

> The wheel of history must not be turned back, and man's advance toward a spiritual life, which began with the primitive rites of initiation, must not be denied. It is

> permissible for science to divide up its field of inquiry and to operate with limited hypotheses, for science must work in that way; but the human psyche may not be so parcelled out. It is a whole which embraces consciousness, and it is the mother of consciousness.

It is not enough to look for and find illness and tend to it:

> The psychotherapist must not allow his vision to be coloured by pathology; he must never allow himself to forget that the ailing mind is a human mind and that, for all its ailments, it unconsciously shares the whole psychic life. He must even be able to admit that the ego is sick for the very reason that it is cut off from the whole, and has lost its connection not only with mankind, but with the spirit.

The mother of consciousness, the psyche, must be joined with the father which is the spirit:

> Ever and again there are human beings who understand what it means that God is their father. The equal balance of the flesh and the spirit is not lost to the world.[13]

Otto Rank had similar points to make in his defection from Freudian ranks, though with a less exuberant assertion of the spirit. His emphasis was, however, like Jung's, on something science could not account for, the will, and alongside the will the urge to immortality which is contained in what he calls the soul. What Rank means by the soul—*der Seele*—is a meeting of psyche and spirit, in which, when we take proper account of it, we may find sanity and salvation. The meeting, within the person, and of person with person, and of individuals and collectivities, has its tensions, but they may work to a good purpose, for all must finally be understood as "phenomena of will," which include "the individual's uncompromising tendencies towards immortality in his dreams, his living, and his works. . . ." How do they achieve a good end? "I think," says Rank, "it is important to bring out the fundamental opposition between the individual will, which seeks to perpetuate itself, and the collective soul, which is immortal, and to show that both are in great degree united in sexuality."

Freud's mistake, according to Rank, was to have conceived "psychic causality" in exclusively historical terms, trying "to explain the present completely in terms of the past. . . ." That simply will not do. It removes the creative force from psychology. Rather than stretching the imagination, such thinking, such procedure, narrows and compresses it. Even if the soul is an illusion, it is a necessary part of our lives, and precisely in the *materia prima* of the imagination, mental images:

> The soul may not exist, and, like belief in immortality, it may prove to be man's greatest illusion; nevertheless it must picture not only the objects, but the content, of psychology, whose objects are not things or facts but ideas and ideologies. And, like our entire human reality, which includes scientific psychology, these same ideologies are products of spiritual belief.

This is how we take "possession" of the things of our world, of ourselves, of the world itself, through the creative imagination. This is how the creative imagination becomes the healing imagination and separates us from neurosis and psychosis:

> The creative person fashions the world according to his conscious, willing ego; the neurotic type interprets it psychologically according to his moralistic guilt ego; and the psychotic identifies himself with it in the sense of his magic, spiritual ego.[14]

Imagination, then, we emphasize, is the creative activity of both psyche and soul. It comes into play in all of our ways of being—in our thinking and feeling, our intuiting, our sensing. It expresses psychic life, which speaks first in images before it speaks in words, the primary imagination making its claims before the secondary can look to dissolve and diffuse and extract them. Without these claims, the salt has lost its flavor and things taste flat, stale, dead. Imagination moves against that loss and its accompanying pains. It presents us with images that simply, quickly occur to us, that pop into our heads, seize our hearts, and all but stop our breathing.[15] Imagination, bridging the gap between the conscious and the unconscious, between primary and secondary process, receives images and works with them. It experiences them creatively, sometimes leads us to produce creative products, a new design or painting, a book, a new way to serve meals or to make love, to create an atmosphere of celebration as we greet a child or surprise a friend with a declaration of feeling.

Imagination yields us images that are familiar and strange, that come bidden or unbidden. A dream image of a skeleton leaning toward us to plant a ghostly kiss may move us to a halloween fantasy, or a bold conscious stance where we demand answers from our image. Who are you, we ask; what do you want? Thus we flesh out the skeleton, reanimate its life and engage it, meeting it head on with our warm-blooded reactions.[16]

The images that appear to us this way, we work over and reconstruct in time. But their first appearance is almost outside the dimension of time. They just happen. They arrive in consciousness from the unconscious, like a wisp of spirit. And they depart the same way, suddenly, just when we want most to hold onto them. Either way, they speak of another life running in us like an underground river-current, always present, never quite seen, exerting influence on us, lapping quietly on our dry ground, rich soil from which things grow.[17] Sometimes we feel held in a moment of stopped time. Sometimes we feel flooded as images knock us over, swamp us, threaten to carry us downstream to the sea, to be lost forever. And so we fear the imagination; we think we could lose our solid ground in it and end up in a mental hospital, as so many of us have. Or perhaps, we think, the river will dry up and leave us parched, scorched, burnt out. Then we must become overly practical, rigid, brittle, as only too many do. That is the threat of psychoanalysis for artists, many of whom fear that the imagination will desert them when it is picked over and taken apart in analysis.[18] Sometimes we fear these dangers so much that we run from the imagination altogether. And then? Then we lose its healing touch.

Imagination heals by building a bridge sturdy enough to link us up, each of us, to the river of being already present in us, to the currents flowing through us and among us in our unconscious life. Imagination is our way back into that space we entered so effortlessly as children when we began, not long after birth, to play. That is what the play of breathing becomes for many religious, a meditation back into the air of effortlessness upon which spiritual exercises thrive. Our child's play with our toes or fingers or our reflection in the glass becomes for us as adults the play between lovers in the touches and exchanges of the body and spirit, and the beholding in our interior life of the mysterious presences bodily and spiritual of the divine. Our play with stuffed animals or dolls that take on richly imagined personalities and histories sustains our grown-up capacity to receive and create images of God that cross and recross the gap between the icons of tradition and our own idiosyncratic pictures. Imagination digs the soil and brings the water so that what comes to us grows. The glorified body lives in our humdrum ordinary flesh. The primary has a home in the secondary and finds its ease there.[19]

In this space between our single unconscious life and our shared conscious life with others, imagination plays and heals. Drawing on images from dreams, taking off from a reverie, playing around with something we have seen or touched or tasted, we create, we find our ease. Perhaps we dream about God coming down the stairs as a woman, middle-aged, a frump in fact. Our imaginations are shocked. So ordinary a god, looking like the most inconsequential woman at the grocery store?[20] Is that what the incarnation means? Does it mean being housed in that kind of flesh? Are we missing a clue, some tell-tale gleam that betrays the divine presence? We hear a man describe a mystical ecstasy, saying it "hit him right between the eyes" and that he "went under." We embroider on it in the space of our own imaginings. Where did he go "under"? Did he enter another place? Was he ecstatic at being released from prosaic being, from being "over" rather than "under"? Imagination at play allows us to dress up, to become angel, witch, animal, to go down into the fearful places, even those of madness, to imagine the great terrifying extremes of life rather than to have to live them. It links river and shore for us. It gives us a space, a passageway, a bridge from the secondary to the primary.

The bridges of the imagination cross the gap between our personal and social lives, between the experience we call subjective because it is so very much our own, so personal, wearing our own odd colors, and the experience that confronts us as objective, standing out there over against us, something others share, with mixed colors. Even the intimate home images of childhood, such as the special window view, the solitary corner, the bedroom lair, rest on a shared imagination. The house, as Jung showed, and after him Bachelard, is the most basic ground-plan of human beings.[21] It is the space we make into our central human dwelling-place. So it is, too, with the fur, hair, hide, skin which mark the boundaries of our living being, contained in the body's housing, presenting itself as a living presence.[22] Even the intimate images that come to us, that really happen to us in the most personal moments of sexual meeting or prayer, have at their source images that we share among us. Images of union—of heaven and earth touching, of circles closing, or light opening, of couples joining, or at the opposite end, images of disjunction, of a relationship sundering, of circles splintered, of light extinguished, of pairs lost to each other, each searching for the other—run through our shared fairy tales, our literature, our myths, our religion. In our own imaginations, we construct bridges to history, to cultures far from ours in time and tone. We recognize and join, even if only in the imagination, the hidden communities of the human family, wherever they may be in time or eternity.

To discover, as the Dalai Lama of Tibet suggests, that our enemy wants the same things that we do—freedom from suffering, happiness—astonishes. Not only are we linked to our enemy, but our suffering at our enemy's hands is joined to that of the Dalai Lama and his Tibet. The Dalai Lama speaks to us of a very specific enemy, one who stole his country and his culture from him and his people, not simply someone who said a nasty word to him or made life difficult at work.[23] Still, large or small, thief of a country or disturber of job-time peace, the enemy takes on a familiar face. We are emboldened by others' endurance of such large suffering to find our way through all the hurts, and especially the petty ones that so often gall. The small suffering anchors the large, lets us see it and not be overwhelmed by its sheer size.

The image that confronts us when our imagination works well may not be ours alone, may not be a modern one only, but also an ancient one, archetypal. Our personal fear of snakes, for example, on which our imagination works overtime, may unearth the primordial snake that beguiles us with an Edenic lure of consciousness. The Kundalini reptile, infusing us with the energies of growth and transformation, may turn out to be the messenger of God mysteriously tempting us into an enlargement of being. A man may discover that his painting of a great multicolored ball that opens up to brilliant whiteness, a picture drawn in an effort to express an enigmatic opening in the soul after a wounding love affair, is an ancient way and a recurrent one, the means alchemists use to describe reaching the female within, the *albedo* stage of "whitening."[24] Daring to receive what happens imaginatively, and working with it, secures a place with others of similar experience, in all ages. We find our community and we contribute to it.

Imagination delivers us over to paradox, to the oblique and contradictory and reconciling lines of the story and the fable, the poem and the play. We join Charles Dickens in contemplating the revelations, the wisdom, the healing humor that can gather around an often improbable name, plucked from the London directory, a Chuzzlewit, a Pecksniff, a Lady Dedlock, a Skimpole, a Jellyby, an Abel Magwitch, a Pumblechook, Merdles and Meagles, Boffins and Veneerings. We make sense out of the secondary imagination's reshaping of the primary in the great tales of the Napoleonic wars, transformed into tutelary ironies in Stendhal's *Charterhouse of Parma,* enlarged to account for all historical forces and then diminished to fit the dimensions of housewifely dreams in Tolstoy's *War and Peace.* We do not need the grafting of consulting-room psychobabble onto

Shakespeare to recognize in Hamlet a psychic disorder which suggests that *he* may be what is rotten in Denmark, as he fails to take up his princely responsibilities. We are grateful for the stubborn bittersweet tragicomic attempt to make dying into a living experience in Hermann Broch's *The Death of Virgil*, and the similarly insistent pushing, probing, sometimes breathless attempt to make the spiritual as familiar to experience as the bodily in T.S. Eliot's *Four Quartets*.[25]

With or without instruction in it, the literary imagination belongs to all of us. All of us have been told stories, tell ourselves stories, make up tales, fables, exemplary cautionings to tell others. Even our lies are grounded in the same primordial soil that produced Aesop, Sophocles, Dante, Dostoevsky, Joyce, the earth of the animating imagination where our psychic life and our spiritual are joined, for better or worse, to the All of Reality.

Our soul is that objectively existing opening in our subjective life that knows about God and goodness and evil, about the transcendent and its reach into the ordinary, into our daily life, into everything. The soul registers with special pleasure our experience of mystery and its source, and wants above all else to know better that source, that ultimate other in our lives. Soul is willingness, even desire, to correspond to that other as it makes itself known to us. The soul's imaginings dwell on who this other is, who this God is that comes to us. Soul asks, Who is there? What do you want of me? How can I be for you, be toward you? Here imagination dips in and out of personal and social history in relation to what God shows us and what the enemies of God reveal. Soul takes off from scripture stories and personal experience to produce meditations in which we enter and speak our needs and listen to the One who summons us and does so through the creative strengths of the imagination. So it is that imagination helps us correspond to grace.[26]

So it is that the imagination heals. How does it do so? What is in it that heals? All these things: its power to frighten us and make us pay attention; its calling into play all our senses; our fearful acknowledgment that its presence in us is the presence of the largeness of Being itself immediately there in all our littleness of being, summoning our active participation in being.

Imagination heals by linking secondary and primary, conscious and unconscious, adult and child, individual and social, personal picture and archetypal symbol, psyche and soul.

Imagination brings an eternity of literary graces to the practice of religion. It changes preaching, makes over praying, enables to teach. It feeds the clergy who feed the people. It includes as a routine observance the evil imaginings of our hearts and our plunges into madness, and finally imagination leads through itself to the place beyond itself, where all our images break, fall silent, and cease in an absence which is both a likeness and a fulfillment. We never reach to the other side, our imagination confirms, by our own efforts alone. We do not ourselves build the bridge to God. Imagination knows that with all its images of imagelessness, even in that empty waiting, that knowing unknowing, our grieving absence is filled with a consoling presence.

Chapter 2

The Gap

Imagination terrifies even when we think of it as a bridge. There is a great opening under the bridge and a gap between the two sides it connects. Even when we conceive of imagination as the connecting link between our conscious and unconscious, between ourselves and others, between our personal and our social existence, between our individual idiosyncratic images of creation and shared pictures of the universe, it still has the power to scare us with its gaps. Instinctively, like beasts with all our antennae bristling, we know we are getting close to something awesome, something more than we had counted on, more than we had hoped for. What will happen when we get out on that bridge and look down? What will we see? Will we be able to proceed?

A man in analysis once described his dread of the gap as like leaving a "picture postcard world" to travel across a rope bridge to some perilous other side.[1] Halfway across, he froze. He knew he could not go back. The postcard was his former life—too small for living, good only for sending a fixed message of a frozen "ideal." There was no room to breathe and be himself. Yet when he looked ahead, there was nothing before him, only a brown barren desert—no inhabitants, no green spots, no water, not even roads. He froze there on his bridge, stopped, and dared to look down. The gap beneath him only widened, deepened into impenetrable depths. He could not move for fear of falling. What do we do when that happens to us?

We do what people have always done, and then have always forgotten, and then have had to learn and relearn. We do three things. We let it happen. We see what happens. We reflect upon what has happened. Those are the necessary steps into the imagination. In this man's case, letting it happen meant letting himself fall. We know that fear of falling is telling us that in some essential way we are ungrounded.[2] We are not fully housed in our own bodies, in the reality of the world, in the depths of the soul. The falling, which we dread, into the upside-down world of the unconscious, is also a rushing to meet and be reconnected with what we have lost and must find again if we are to grow our roots downward. Treated literally, such a fear is dangerous, pulling us closer and closer to the railing of the bridge, dizzying us with vertigo, as when we look down from the height of a great building, hurling us down a long steep flight of stairs. We could go over at any time.

Looked at imaginatively, however, the fear of falling takes on a positive power, that of a central symbol in our lives, one that links us to unconscious forces seeking the center of being, the one that consciously we have despaired of finding.[3] Falling, symbolically, is reaching out to the core we have lost. It is a movement in us that transforms an ego that has run out of possibilities, sometimes even of hope. If we can fall imaginatively, we do not literally have to fall apart. Imagination can save our lives.

Letting our imagination be is both not so simple as it sounds and much simpler than we would expect. What we are after is noninterference. We must refuse to be hasty. We must put aside perfectionist or utopian pictures. There is nowhere we must get to; there are no prescribed images that must appear. We sit quietly, as if in meditation, waiting to see who will come through the door. We let it be, a *passion* that in very small ways can enter imaginatively into the great passion of Jesus. We do not do; we are. We allow whatever will to come to us and open ourselves to it, whether it be in sight, sound, touch, taste or smell.

Such a letting be may involve a great risk, for we are consenting to what is and renouncing any expediency of purpose. We want to see what is there and what is not, instead of imposing what we want. We will not rush off to make immediate use of it. Beholding is enough. Such a letting be is akin to the spiritual exercises that simply proclaim being in its particularities, the *this*ness of things, no large abstractions, no great generalizations. It is this moment, this picture, this feeling that we take in and concentrate upon. In its small special concentration of being, we can find all we are looking for, even "God's Grandeur," as Gerard Manley Hopkins did. It all begins with one image, startling in its ordinariness, and moves to another equally prosaic and moving.

> The world is charged with the grandeur of God.
> It will flame out, like shining from shook foil;
> It gathers to a greatness, like the ooze of oil
> Crushed. Why do men then now not reck his rod?

"I mean foil in its sense of leaf or tinsel," Hopkins explained in a letter to another poet, "and no other word whatever will give the effect I want. Shaken goldfoil gives off broad glares like sheet lightning and also, and this is true of nothing else, owing to its zigzag dents and creasings and network of small many-cornered facets, a sort of forked lightning too."

Hopkins was, like the medieval theologian Duns Scotus, "who of all men most sways my spirits to peace," haunted by the *this*ness of things. He looked for the universal in the particular, and in his own works and those of the figures most precious to him he offers us precise instruction in how to let things be. Scotus is for him "Of reality the rarest-veinèd unraveller." Another rare figure for Hopkins, the composer Henry Purcell, has not, like "other musicians . . . given utterance to the moods of man's mind," but "beyond that, uttered in notes the very make and species of man as created both in him and in all men generally." The prized achievement is that something so large can be contained in something so small. Our very being can be "uttered in notes." That is how we unravel reality, a note at a time. We are caught by all that stands behind the shining light that bursts from shaken metallic foil, by the marvels of pattern and color that form in the undulating oozings of oil that have been crushed into the ground by foot or wheel or whatever. We stop. We admire. We imagine and we understand: "meaning motion fans fresh our wits with wonder."[4]

In letting be, we agree to the blurring of the usual categories of discrimination and open ourselves to the shock of wonder and joy. We might, for example, like the painter Cézanne, open our eyes and see all around us ". . . nothing but a great coloured undulation. . . . An irradiation and glory of colour . . . a coloured state of grace."[5] We might feel the mass of things, their embodied presence. A stone impresses itself so firmly upon us as we look at it, it almost makes an indentation in our flesh. Waiting, watching, opening to things, we do not prescribe or impose, we receive. Images arise to surprise and fascinate us. They may come from the outside world and build on its facticity, so that, for example, a tree at dusk is both itself and the carrier of the resplendent blackness we call the night. A shadowed tree limb exceeds its ordinary spatial limits and promises to take us through its breaks and shadows into the very center of the dark, to reveal the darkness of the dark at its source. But always, it is this tree, this limb, this shadow, this gathering of darkness. It is the particularity of things that the imagination feeds upon and grows with.

Letting be this way is not a hapless passivity. We do not ever just pass by or let anything just come past us, whether person, object, place, or event. The very air is alive with meaning, "Wild air, world-mothering air," as Hopkins called it in that remarkable poem "The Blessed Virgin compared to the Air we Breathe." But we must remain alert in this soft sweet charged exercise of being. We must concentrate. We must fill the gaps of inattention with our own heedings. Fourteen-hundred years ago, Gregory the Great summoned us to this way of letting be, called us to attention. "Those things which are full of marvels for an investigation deeper than we can reach," he reminds us, "have become cheap from custom in the eyes of man. . . ." The examples are many and dramatic:

> . . . if a dead man is raised to life, all men spring up in astonishment, yet every day one that had no being is born, and no man wonders, though it is plain to all, without doubt, that it is a greater thing for that to be created which was without being than for that which had being to be restored. . . . Because the dry rod of Aaron budded, all men were in astonishment; . . . every day a tree is produced from the dry earth, and no

> man wonders. . . . Five thousand men were filled with five loaves. . . . every day the grains of seed that are sown are multiplied in a fulness of ears, and no man wonders. . . . All wondered to see water once turned into wine. Every day the earth's moisture, being drawn into the root of the vine, is turned by the grape into wine, and no man wonders. Full of wonder then are all the things which men never think to wonder at, because . . . they are by habit become dull to the consideration of them. . . .[6]

When our imagination is confronted by the particularities of the world around us, we can do wonderful things with them and even for them, if we have not "by habit become dull to the consideration of them." When images arise spontaneously from within us, they may be all the more startling because they issue from outside our knowing. They often come from our unknowing, our unconscious. These images may frighten. They may also fix our attention. They are usually oddly mixed combinations of personal peculiarities and familiar human themes. A man sees on his inner screen, for example, an image of Christ with clawed feet. It captures with surprising simplicity not only his own crippled feet but also the animal layer of the divine. What good is a god-image if it does not put a finger—a foot—precisely on our personal suffering and especially that which makes us feel ashamed. A god-image tough enough to survive always reaches down to the instinctual layer. As long as the animals are still in our religion, Jung said, it is healthy and alive. When the animals leave, the religion is dying. Images that arise from the unconscious, according to Jung, "are meant to attract, to convince, to fascinate, and to overpower. They are created out of the primal stuff of revelation and reflect the ever-unique experience of divinity. That is why they always give man a premonition of the divine while at the same time safeguarding him from immediate experience of it."[7] The point is that something has arrived. We need to get to see it and to know it.

To see what arrives is the next step here. We must look hard, daringly, using our mind, our memory, our sense of the past, our feelings. We must ask, Who is there? The spiritual risk that began in letting be what is there, and what is not, intensifies. Our seeing enters a zone of communication that challenges common sense. Subject and object blur in their indwelling. We feel our own *I* to be there with a *not-I.* What we see mediates to us things we do not see, but in such a way that what we know, we experience immediately, without intervention. Yet, as Jung says, the image itself clothes the raw experience, both protecting and making the primal stuff accessible. The image acts as a sort of picture frame, marking off the reality it points to from ordinary daily things and making it palpable. Poems and religious rituals do the same, as a regular session of therapy may do or a set time devoted to prayer and meditation. The framing image makes the work of our imagination safe.[8]

We can let go now within the image to concentrate on its content, even risk losing ourselves for a moment. The image reminds us that it is real enough as an image, but no more than an image, and thus makes it safe for us to lose ourselves in its reality. We can be both concentrated and without ulterior motive, settling without embarrassment into a wide-open stare, or avid listening, or open-pore sensation to the formless reality, the silent reality, the unseen reality toward which the image steers us. We go *per visibilia ad invisibilia,* as St. Paul sums it up, through the seen into the unseen.[9] For example, a nun finds in William Blake's picture of the Trinity a missing piece of her own personal psychology, an iconic translation of transference experience in psychoanalysis, and a new aspect of the divine. The image frames a time-space continuum where all these bits of experience collide and open upon a new and unguessed unity. In Blake's sketch the God-figure hovers over the wounded Son, crouching almost on his haunches, with outstretched arms forming the Cross. The Son leans on the Father with all his weight, and the Father bears the burden in intimate, even undignified squat.[10] The patient was riveted. Framed in this image was all the tough-minded support, the psychological and physical backing, that she had missed in her own father. When she reached to lean upon him, she just fell down. No haunches, no strong arms, no squatting holding presence. So she never leaned. She held herself up. In the transference experience, she dared to lean and was repeatedly amazed that the analyst did not fall over. She did not have to protect the analyst but could depend on her, trusting that she would fend for herself. In this colliding of her aggression and her dependence, she saw God in a new way: God was strong enough, specifically fatherly enough, to take whatever vigorous impulses or inclinations she wanted to give in to. She did not have to protect God, but could let go fully, could let be, all the way to what was there and what might not be there when she prayed. Her need always to maintain herself loosened up and God got through. In the image of the protecting Father, strong and loving enough to bear the full weight of the wounded Son, she found she could yield to all her own energies—her excitement, her anger, her desire. She could let herself go, with freedom, to the sheer bigness of the divine other. The formless power exceeded all her forms. She could risk it because of what the image of the Trinity provided.

Imagination is tough. It is naturally open. It wants to see everything. That is a large part of its healing power. It includes the daunting negative as well as the uplifting positive. It naturally renounces denial. It looks to include the wildly spiraling off-center event as well as the grounding, centering one. Imagination instructs us that seeing what is there means looking directly into off-center events and the gaps, like the man frozen on the bridge or the nun peering into imagelessness. When we consent to let be and look at what is there and what is not, we see crowding onto us, into us, all the things we usually deny, all that we screen out of our lives. Bits of hoping that we have given up, or lost, rush in. We acknowledge again our lively greed for money, food, things, status, power, sex. We admit to mute despair when we have just given up our hopes, unable to dare anything out of the way, even to wish for things. We do not deny a crude ambition that would just place us first in whatever is being ranked, first to get attention, first to succeed, first to prevail, always to be first in line. We see our own wolfish desires, our seething contempt for others, petty meannesses and peevish refusals to respond at all. Fear, envy, anger writhe in us like snakes in a pit, it may be, and we say Yes, it is so. We see our own inertia, that distancing fog—"I can't stir myself to wake up and look at you"—that alternates with all the raw self-aggrandizement. We look into the gap between what we want and what we get, between what we ambition and what we realize, between where we should be and where we are, between the ideal and the reality. We see the positive and negative collide. We recognize that they live next to each other.

The gap is more than personal. It is not in us alone, and a lively working imagination will tell us so. The gap is a metaphor for all our days; it describes all of life. There is a gap between what nations promise, hope for, strive for and what they accomplish. Just as in art, the product falls short of the vision of the artist. That is the inevitable suffering of the artist.[11] The gap is there between us, any of us, all of us, even in our most intimate meetings. Ecstasy is often described as that fleeting fraction of a moment when two do really become one in sexual climax, or in perfect mutual communication, or in the spark of mystical union of the soul and the divine.

If we risk looking at what our imagination sets before us—the odd snippet of an image, of a sense-impression, of an interior understanding, a flash of color, a dog's wet nose, a cat's purring, the sound of falling rain, the thunder of gunshots, the sudden accession of meaning of a language—we will be led to look into the gap that exists between the image and the thing itself. We will soon see that the gap is itself paradoxical, constantly there after we cross it and close it and all the more open because the closing depends on the gap's existence in the first place. Film is the best modern example of that.

The gap is one of the major reasons film has such a hold on our imaginations. It is the psychological and spiritual accuracy of its hop-skip-and-jump presentation of human experience that makes its case so persuasive that even a wretched script, ineptly enacted and tonelessly directed, will keep us in our seats as long as the camera-work is professional. When the actors are familiar, they can fill the gaps just by the slightest facial movement or rearrangement of body. They react for us, and with all the more meaning when we have watched them many times. They signal, as no panning shot over the villain's getaway route can do, that the posse is catching up, or that the villain is getting away, or that a monstrous crash is about to happen. When we get beyond such simple gap-filling into the interstices of personality that an actor's face or body can point to and close over for us, we see how powerful the inflated images of film are and how well they mirror, in gigantic blow-up, the events of psyche and soul.

That is what Alfred Hitchcock drew from actors like Cary Grant and Ingrid Bergman, James Stewart, Grace Kelly, and Vera Miles. Working with simple suspense scenarios, Hitchcock created a geography of the Gothic so compelling that it was possible to believe his actors were really at the center of things, that life was one continuous melodrama peopled with spies, psychotics, and elegant virgins of uncertain age just waiting for the right charmer, usually a professional thief, to relieve them of their sexual anxiety. Silly, filled with coincidences that do not stand up to close examination, and with moments of sadistic exploitation of the audience, such film-making is not easy to dismiss, for it tutors in the art of the gap. It helps us to make sense of what directors like François Truffaut or Luis Buñuel or Ingmar Bergman can do with the blanks in human experience where anxiety is born and can be shown to grow up into disaster or something better. The better in the work of these masters of the gap may often just be barely suggested, but it is unmistakably present.

Buñuel does it with a wry Surrealist humor, in which, for example, a pompous gathering of bourgeois is ritualized by seating them on toilets around a dining table and turning eating into a solitary vice. For Bergman, living in the anxiety-breeding gaps can make equal in intensity a woman's period, the news that China has exploded a hydrogen bomb, and the incestuous sexuality of sisters in a totalitarian society, and suggest that religious faith can be drawn from dwelling in such cleavages of feeling and propriety at least as successfully as from the formulas of churches. For Truffaut, every film is a self-questioning, on his part, on the part of his actors, on ours in the audience. Whether his characters are young boys or young men or young women who draw men to them with such allure that two of them would rather share one woman than chance losing her, the impulse is to wonder, to feel defeated, to hope, but never to give up the reality of decent possibility, even at the edge of despair, even in time of Nazi occupation. The gap remains.[12]

We, in the movie theater, do not know how long the flight of stairs is as a villain prepares to mount. We have no precise idea of the distance between cars or gangs of men on horses in a chase. The camera creates an image of threat by making its gaps. We see the foot on the stairs and then we see a man or woman in bed sweating to hear the unfamiliar frightening noise that smashed into his or her sleep. We do not know how far the train station is from the taxi rushing down the street to get to it before the train pulls out, or the exact size of the city the cops must cover to catch the robbers. We cannot possibly know where the dirt roads turn as the posse pursues its prey or the gallant innocent victims run for their lives in mountains they have never seen before. The gap can widen the tension or triumphantly relieve it, either by capture or escape. Our unconscious, in this film-fed world, is dense with such pictures. A man in analysis describes his plight with a film image of a train stopped in a train station, with all its cars gathered together, but not hooked up. It stopped there because it had nowhere to go. Now he knew he had such a train, was such a train. The parts of his life had been brought together in analysis; but they were still unconnected. The image surprised both patient and analyst when he suddenly grew anxious over the idea of closing the gaps between the cars. What looked like the next comfortable task, the coupling of parts, turned out to be the most dreaded. To close the gaps by connection felt like extinction, no space to be his ownmost self but instead to become like any old train that ought to get on its way. The image gave the analysis new energy when it showed that the gaps, the multiple disconnections, had served to protect the man's hidden true self hiding under compliance with persons, with society, with his job.

Gaps persist. They can be positive or negative, most often negative when we deny they are there and most likely to be positive when we acknowledge them and enlarge ourselves to embrace them, like an instructive film director. We must, like directors, present ourselves with all the facts, with all the data of the imagination we can dredge up, with as much as we can know about what is at issue. It is like peace talks, for example, which go so much better if the talkers see the widely different meanings their different cultures give to words like "power" and "freedom." The gaps may not be perfectly bridged, but at least they are acknowledged or rejected. So it is with preaching, which will only reach its listeners if the preacher thinks about the gap between the meanings scripture discloses and those the average parishioner harbors. D.W. Winnicott goes so far as to say we cannot be original except in relation to tradition, which is to say we only strike freshness when we admit to consciousness all that we can of the words and beliefs of the past which have shaped us.[13]

We see the truth of that most keenly in our religious lives. A gap exists between the images that have come down to us in doctrine and liturgy and our personal god-images.[14] Often we are not even aware of our own pictures of God, but they operate in us anyway somewhere below consciousness. Something assumes central focus and dominant importance in our psyches and around that point all else revolves, whether we consciously acknowledge it or not. It may be a fear. It may be a drinking problem. It may be a child or a wished-for mate. It may be our job. It may be a picture of God that has come to us in a dream, or that we have harbored in varying degrees of consciousness since childhood. Whatever it is, that god-image bears the particular stamp of our personality, our culture and background, our time in history. For example, a six-year-old boy found his picture of God in a television image, the drawing of a face in profile crowned with fiery red hair. We know such pictures, we feel their mark, even if we do not understand them. They are numinous to us, bearing toward us the power and presence of the All.

In prayer such images pop up frequently and persist even though traditional prayer manuals advise against taking them seriously. That warning is a mistake, we think, inspired by fear.[15] The fact is, most people are afraid of such images. They try to dismiss them, hoping to get back on the rails of prescribed spiritual exercises, not guessing, as the man with the unhooked railroad cars did, that the gaps between personal and official images for God may well be where the precious blood of life is to be found.

We may have reason to be afraid of our god-images. Some seem extreme. A woman trying to claim all of her female sexuality dreams of a damaged woman who exposes herself, "all of her private parts," to the dreamer, in doing so "trusting me," the dreamer adds. "That was Christ," she concluded at last, and felt deeply touched, healed by the image. Another woman, in sobs, describes the joyful swimming motions of her unborn baby on the sonoscope, a "free spirit, a joyous being," that she had aborted. She saw her own promising self there, an image even of Being itself looping upward and downward and around the screen. A third woman dreams of a Buddha constructed from the ordinary things of life—a car, a bit of food, a house, lakes, roads, buildings. It conveys to her that the mysterious ineffable composes itself and shows itself through the mundane.

Afraid of them or not, such personal god-images are important to us. We hide them and yet we consult them. We carry them with us always. Often, we fail to bring them forward to meet the official god-images offered by tradition, feeling instead only the wide gap that separates the personal images from the consecrated ones. What is a man to do, when his meditations on the Christ-figure confront him with a huge tiger of thick lustrous fur? How does that cohere with Jesus meek and mild? The religious imagination always will insist on taking that particular tack. It makes us ask how the old official pictures of God touch, inform, confront our personal god-images, and how our own images touch, confront, inform those of tradition.

Out of the gap between those two sets of images grows the special work of the religious imagination and the dissipation of our fears. A fearful people will ignore the gap by trying to wipe out the personal, denying the odd off-center god-image that appears when they let themselves be in prayer, burying it in the darkness of repression. This is a great loss. We lose the fresh new life, the accrual of being, that our images could contribute to tradition. Without our own distinct and often very fine images, as Winnicott puts it, ". . . crude expression of appetite and of sexuality and of hate would be the rule. Fantasy in this way proves to be the human characteristic, the stuff of socialisation and of civilisation itself."[16] Are these private god-images any more strange than Ezekiel's vision of wheels within wheels or John's image of eating the "bitter" scroll?

Gaps in religion should not lead to losses but to openings.[17] That is what we see in the woman examining the connection between her image of Jesus Christ as a vulnerable woman reclaiming her lost female parts and the gospel Christ, who speaks to all women as equals. The opening here is a spiritual weaving of the strands of sexual life, out of which a new piece of fabric is made available to deepen the tradition, not to discard it. Many woman saints did just that, finding Christ as mother, drawing from his wounds a kind of menstrual blood-food for the birth of the spirit.[18]

If we try to close the gap from the other side alone, exultantly embracing our own god-images and altogether rejecting tradition, we must also lose. We have our own images and they are precious, but they need much more nourishment than they can bring with them to grow large enough to house the spirit. Our images are little. Tradition is large. It is crammed with a wonderful range of pictures of God—as seamstress sewing clothes for Adam and Eve, as designer prescribing the style of the ephod, as architect designing the ark and the temple, as dinner-party host, as wind, as fire and rock and water. We need such a storehouse of images to elaborate our own views.

Without access to tradition, preachers concoct sermons, however moving and interesting, which do not reach beyond their own experiences in prayer, in marriage or divorce, in the war, in training in seminary or hospital or prison. We do not hear the gospel. Worse still, without acknowledging tradition, we all tend to identify with our god-images and want everyone else to identify with them too. Everything, in this reductive reading of religion, is a self-object.[19] We push our personal image of God into the public arena to become the new official god. That is nothing but theological despotism, a perversion of the imagination, no less coercive and persecutory than the Inquisition.

How then to live with the gap? How can we cope with the unavoidable separation in religious life between our experiences of the divine and the God revelation and tradition bring to us? Without a tutored and practised imagination we cannot risk the gap.

The third step in imagination is systematic reflection on what we have let be and on what comes to us as a result. Amazing things happen. A remarkable quality of self-experience, the experience of one's own special being connected to all being, sets in. Imagination helps us sort out what comes to us. Its healing power consists in this receiving and turning over and looking through all the images and fantasy elaborations of experience in our bodies, in relationship to others, in our world, in our attempts to reach to the center of life. We receive and turn over, rather than repress. Thus handled, even terrible agonies of body or disintegrating anxieties of mind and soul can be lived with. Healing is sorting through and linking up. It means finding and connecting to symbols that bring and knit together the disparate elements of experience.[20] This is what making whole means, a collecting and recollecting, allowing our memories to bead together all the bits of past, present, and future into the connected necklace of the personal. "Continuity of being is health."[21] An alive center in us responds to and makes use of, rather than just reacts to, or defends against, the pressure of others, the impingements of the past, the intrusion of uninvited persons or events, the constant presence of the gap.

The past is alive in the present, but we must approach it over a gap. A symbolic tension exists in persons, in rooms, in houses. There are signs to be read, revelations to be made. If we see the gap as a gap in our understanding, not an unbridgeable gulf, we will learn much to our advantage, as the old fortune-tellers used to put it. T. S. Eliot makes this appeal in the voices of a chorus of aunts and uncles, sisters and brothers-in-law who are the fateful pursuers in his Christianized version of Aeschylus, *The Family Reunion*.

In an old house there is always listening, and more is heard
than is spoken.
And what is spoken remains in the room, waiting for the
future to hear it.
And whatever happens began in the past, and presses hard
on the future.
The agony in the curtained bedroom, whether of birth or
of dying,
Gathers in to itself all the voices of the past, and projects
them into the future.

For Eliot, all that has been in some sense still is with us—high-pitched voices outside the house, mowing, old animals, the sounds of wood being chopped and singing. So are some less attractive things:

The moment of sudden loathing
And the season of stifled sorrow
The whisper, the transparent deception
The keeping up of appearances
The making the best of a bad job
All twined and tangled together, all are recorded.[22]

It isn't a magic act, though there is magic in it. We do not exactly snatch these pictures, these recorded images and sounds, from the air, though they hover over us like the sounds and images that coalesce into the words and pictures of radio and television. They are in our aunts' and uncles' and parents' and grandparents' recollections. They are, as Eliot also liked to point out, in old photographs, in books of reminiscences. They are in the vast archetypal world that an intimate relationship, which at its best is an observant relationship, opens up to us.

We pay attention. We follow people in our lives as we do the people on the screen, and just as we conclude without great effort that the person seen at the bottom of the stairs in one frame who in the next frame is at the top has made his or her way up the stairs, so we look to read the movements, the gestures, the postures of those around us. Better still, we find a large symbolic drama in them and their setting and ours. As the Cubists have so tellingly made clear in their gatherings of all the elements in the setting of a table, wallpaper, chair fabric, newspaper, wine decanter, fruit, there are endless details, and rewarding ones, to be brought into the gallery of experience. We look and we see. We take in the symbols of our spaces in the precise terms of our lives, just as Picasso and Braque and Juan Gris did in the exact terms of their canvases and papers, in the flattenings of the two-dimensional picture plane which is the natural life of canvases and papers. Everything, just about, looked at this way, has symbolic meaning, form as well as content. And everything is connected, at least in our understanding, even unhooked railroad cars.

Making symbolic links changes our own perceiving. We move from representation to presentation, from unhearing listening and unseeing viewing to heedful responses. The image acts as a doorway and we go through it knowing there is an I doing that as well as a You ready to respond. The experience of the *I*ness of our selves usually comes in moments of joy or pleasure in sharply pointed states of being. We know an intense sense of being alive in our own body, there, with a lack of self-consciousness and a lack of mindfulness, plunged into a keen sense of presence to self and what is around and beyond ourselves. Even the air glows. We feel the quivering of being all around us, like heat shimmering above a hot pavement. Sometimes gravity seems to shift from being down below, under us, holding us up, to a force all around us, as if we were held again in the life-giving fluid of the womb before birth. Subject and object join but not to annihilate each other.[23] Rather, separation of self and other is transfigured into interpenetration. We feel gratitude for the plenitude of what is, even Eliot's moments of "sudden loathing" and seasons of "stifled sorrow." Such simple happiness in being is not built on the denial of suffering and want, but holds them in place, and with contemplative respect.

The I-feeling, the not-I, the You-feeling all persist. A sign of the power and health of the imagination is an increased capacity to put ourselves into the thoughts and feelings of others and to receive their movements, their gestures and postures, like their words, with serious heedful consideration. The people and the images they bring with them, and the working of our imagination that folds them and refolds them into our awareness, give us a sense that what we thought we were doing may in fact be something that is being done in and through us by others.

Our images, which seem so insistently personal to us, so much of our time and our place, may also open us to timeless pictures and enactments in the psyche. As a seashell may lead us in our imaginings into the depths of the sea, the images of our little personal spaces may lead us into the great deeps where whatever has been in the past remains a perpetual possibility, "and presses hard," as Eliot says, "on the future." We discern the pattern-making power of the imagination, where persons take shape and a You comes to meet an I or a We.[24]

Illusion is a necessary structure of thought about the "Wholly Other," Paul Ricoeur says, in which "the sacred is an area of combat." We may be caught between signs of absolute otherness, of the unconditioned God, and signs which even in the sacred simply reflect our culture.[25] We must choose here to make a deeper sense of our images, to let them take us where they and we are meant to go.

Our particular images may bring us into an imageless center which we could not reach except by these particularities and which we must lose if we do not move from image to image, from present to past and future, from undenying observation to symbolic linkings. That was the genius of Job, that he identified and disidentified, held on to old images and attitudes and understandings until he arrived in the presence of Yahweh and then could let himself go over to the vastly unfamiliar but unmistakably real threshold of the new. Then he, who had shaken his fist in the face of the Lord, having used his imagination so heedfully, became the one to speak to the same Lord for his less conscious, less open, unheeding friends.[26]

Turning over our images brings us to the edge of the known. It restores the being we lost to us, like the woman who needed to accept her female parts in the image of a womanly Jesus. It fills us with being we can embrace, like the man who had to look beyond the railroad cars to the gaps between them. Imagination moves us to feel moved by something clearly within us that nonetheless is not us, that comes to us as an I and addresses us as a You. In Heidegger's handsome phrase, we are asked to become "shepherds of being."[27]

Chapter 3

Madness

It is an unfortunate tradition, consecrated in prayer manuals and works of spirituality, to treat imagination as something to be conquered, dispelled, put aside as a hindrance to the concentration required for spiritual meditation and contemplation. Imagination interrupts, distracts, carries us off into reveries far away from the God we address, we are cautioned.[1] In fact, however, imagination has and always has had a central place in prayer. We cannot conduct a spiritual life without it, as the lush imagery of St. John of the Cross, who counsels us to eschew imagery, so amply demonstrates.[2] The giants of the spiritual life attest to this. Even when we go beyond images we use an image, the one of imagelessness.

For all that, imagining continues to stir fears. If we dare to trace the fears to their source, we will see that in some way we connect imagining with madness. Imagination indulged could derange. What if we told others that we often ruminate about what it would be like to live as a member of the opposite sex? Forget that Patrick White, a novelist of genius, wrote *The Twyborn Affair* out of precisely that fantasy, in which his leading character is first a woman, then a man, then a different woman, and finally still another man before his death.[3] The brilliance of the book opens to us the different departure-points of the woman-man and the man-woman. But that is only a novel, after all. What if we shared our repeating sexual fantasy, the basic plot that spans decades of our lives? What if we spoke of our necessary ritual in going to bed, our repeated formulaic prayers, without which we find it almost impossible to lie down and sleep? What if we admitted to our own awareness the traces of unlived life at the edge of imagination, what did not happen that we dearly hoped would, the wishes we buried? We squirm at the thought of such revelations.

Imagination is associated with madness, as in the fantastic roles demented people claim for themselves—the agent of the devil to kill blond women the "Son of Sam" thought himself, the woman in the psychiatric ward claiming to be the mother of the savior, the political leader who plays the role of chieftain of the master race and persuades millions that he is the one and they are the other. Such imaginings grip a person totally, overrun any ego caution, and eliminate what Freud called the procrastinating function of thought. What is human in a person disappears under the onslaught of a collective impersonal role and accounts for much of the violence we do to one another.

A parent may try to fit a child to his unlived fantasy, coercing his son to realize what he, the father, has neglected. When imagination captures us, does not heal but harms, it is because we have not penetrated to the center of the images that hold us in their grip and faced their power squarely. A husband acts resentfully to his wife undergoing menopause because that fact challenges his unexamined fantasy about himself as a swinging man fitted out with a young and sexy woman. Even when he comes to regret this attitude and to feel remorse for his lack of sympathy for his wife, healing requires his turning over in detail the fantasy which holds him in thrall. When a young woman aspires in her imagination to become a great actress, she needs to examine the image of herself she holds to see if it is not really a dream of becoming famous and rich, with the freedom to work when and where and how she likes, that animates her, or whether the image turns more closely on the richness of the art of the drama, its great texts, its extraordinary craft. That would mean long hours in rehearsals, tours with lesser companies, the endless rearranging of one's daily schedule and employment around auditions, working backstage at menial jobs, an endless going to acting classes. The images that guide us are powerful. How we relate to them differentiates healing from harm.

We have used imagination and fantasy interchangeably. In the matter of madness and the imagination we need to describe these terms more precisely. Fantasy partakes of our unconscious life, what Freud called primary process and Jung nondirected thinking.[4] This kind of fantasy thought consists of streams of images that arise spontaneously to elaborate on the experiences and meanings our bodily functioning throws up. Fantasies collect around body zones, such as the mouth, with its eating, sucking, biting, chewing, and spitting out, with all that they stand for that goes far beyond food. The same is true for other dominant body zones, as in the holding in or gushing forth of urine and stools. Around this part of the body, images of collecting, amassing, and manufacturing a product out of ourselves congregate. There is the capacity in a man, as Winnicott puts it, to swank and strut in the phallic phase and to push on, push in, and put out a seed for new life in the genital phase; in a woman, the capacity to hide away, keep things secret, then bring forth the flesh of her flesh in the blood-mysteries of the genital phase.[5]

Fantasies happen—and happen, and happen again. They express our psychic life, the language of which is filled with images from the outside world, brought inside to be shaped and reformed, images that now find their own spontaneous life inside us, images that we fashion to our needs and then expel back into the world. The images are both personal and archetypal. They may wear our own distinctive colors but they occur to people everywhere.[6]

Though shaped individually by circumstances of family, clan, tribe, culture, and history, the themes are unmistakably the same, and have been for millennia. To see, for example, in a work of pre-Periclean sixth-century archaic Greek art in a tiny statue called "Mourning Woman," the familiar gestures of arms thrown back, elbows bent, hands gripping the sides of the head, back arched, breast exposed in anguish, is to recognize gestures and attitudes we might have seen in our own time at the funeral of a beloved person. We are linked with all womankind, past, present, future. This is a soul-sorrow that will not be consoled, and it is all the mourning that comes with living and loving.

What is so precious about the image is that it always offers us access to shared human experience through the particularity of the picture. Instead of abstractions about life, generalizations that we coerce ourselves or others to fit, these images give us the real thing, the special one, through which we can reach to understand and to share. The images that touch us in our fantasies are not only potent in personal terms, expressing our own particular experience of what is happening now in our bodies, and what happened before that we collect and recollect in memory; they bespeak the continuity of the race, of past, present and future, at the same time that they form an inner history for us, our defining space of the spirit, our interiority. These images, personal and very much of our world, are also timeless and powerful in evoking experiences from across centuries and civilizations, that shape us from the inside out. A woman priest, successful in her calling, half knows that being overweight and fat contributes to her success. She says her obesity not only knocks out a complicating sexuality between her and her parishioners but senses it does more than she can put into words. Perhaps it is an ancient great-mother image that her size conjures up, that ample plenitude of being from which we all get born, which her overabundant flesh bodies forth.[7]

These images, body-based, personal, and archetypal, that fantasy puts before us streaming from the unconscious, bring us closer to our deep-down realities. They span the gap between conscious and unconscious. They reach toward the primary and the primordial.[8] Fantasy pictures defy our conscious rules of space and time, cause and effect. Spaces intertwine and time condenses to an ever-present now that includes past and future. The images express our experience in recognizable ways, but they do not refer to a precise external reality nor purport any specific goal to be achieved. When we passively behold fantasy, we drift and dream on its waves, surprised to see where they carry us. We are suddenly back in a favorite corner of a childhood house, in a secret hiding place in a tree, in a mad feeling where time disappears and buildings undulate and enlarge and diminish, where flowers talk and odd but not frightening animals greet us. If we actively confront these streams of images, work to receive one or two, and respond to them with our own conscious objections, awe, or arguments we may come to the breath-stopping realization of just how independent of our conscious control such images are. They have a life of their own. They push at us. They talk back. They will not be manipulated. When a woman confronts in fantasy a great ugly thug who senselessly wrecks the tables and chairs inside a roadside diner where she has stopped, terrorizing everyone, she is amazed first to discover herself yelling at him indignantly and then to hear the thug screaming back at her. "What do you think you're doing?" she cries. "You're terrifying me! Cut it out!" He roars back: "There is no other way you'll ever notice me! You don't give a damn about my existence, but go on as if I'm really not here. All that's left is terrorizing. Now you notice me!" A screaming match ensues. Finally both sides of the woman, her civilized conscious self and her undomesticated, unconscious one that is filled with unusable primitive aggression, one female and the other portrayed as male, meet as equals, at the very least in volume.

Our fantasies consist of streams of images drawn from everything that happens to us, to which we react passively or actively. Our imagination equips us to go beyond this, to a creative psychic activity. Imagination does have its autonomous side, much like the fantasies that just happen to us. But imagination, by its very terms of existence, means conscious willingness, a consenting participation in image-life and work to make something of it. This in turn means digesting, contemplating images, then sorting them out, distributing and experiencing them in creative living.[9] That may or may not issue forth in the products of art—paintings, musical compositions, plays, poetry, novels. It does assure us both a capacity for living that is body-based and personal, and a participation in shared archetypal images.

Why then should we fear that imagination might lead us into madness? Because it is so full, covers so much, has such insistent power. It touches body and emotion, our sense of identity, our life with others, everything. We fear imagination because of the power of images to change our bodies as they stimulate our appetites, bring erections, wetness, and orgasms, make our stomachs heave and our bowels loosen. Images seem both to fracture and to mend the self. We imagine, for example, that our real self lives in a box over our heads and that what the world sees is not the real self but a disguise that veils us, perhaps even from ourselves. When we finally get back the missing piece of ourself that, like the keystone in an arch, holds everything together, we can trust being exposed. The real self has come down to join the rest. Imagination has the power to perform such feats, personal and collective. It can set armies marching and activate Gestapo-like secret police. It can invade our bedroom at three in the morning and drag us from our beds. It can start wars; it can end them.

Imagination harms rather than heals, starts rather than ends wars, when we fail to use it and are used by it instead. We go mad in two ways, then. We either come too close to the gap that imagination spans and tumble in, falling captive to our images, becoming them instead of imagining them, or we move too far away from the gap, rejecting imagination altogether. Thus we either drown in our images or die for lack of their life-giving waters. Either way, we reject the reality of the image as image.

Our refusal to use our imagination costs us not only imagination but reality. For unacknowledged, unreceived fantasies invade reality all the more demandingly and eventually usurp its place. A husband tries to coerce his wife to fit his fantasy-image at the expense of her actual body and psyche in menopause. A woman loses the theatrical career she covets to daydreams of becoming rich and famous. Failure to do the work of the imagination, which is really play, loses us the symbolic world where one thing stands for another, and delivers us instead over to the literal world where this equates with that, where we identify with our unacknowledged fantasies instead of seeing them and accepting them as what they are, no more, no less. Then we do not simply feel like a victim, isolated in our imagination from everyone's understanding and beleaguered by their rejection; we become a victim who victimizes others. They in turn fill out our fantasies. They really reject and persecute us as we see them. Falling into the gap and identifying with our images in this way is what produces the sniper shooting at innocent students, the man who shoots cyanide into supermarket yogurt or pain-killers, the ex-soldier who guns down first-graders because he cannot tell the difference between Oriental school-children playing at recess and Viet Cong guerrillas.

Unlived fantasy and unused imagination burgeon within us and must be put somewhere. We project the unreceived and unexamined images onto our neighbors, near and far. We feel persecuted. We know that there are people out there ready to get us. Those alien to us become enemies to us. We collectivize them. They become our scapegoats now not in imagination, but in fact, in witch-hunts, flagrant discrimination against "those" of different color, race, religion, sex, mental capacity, or wealth.[10] At our worst, we feel so abused and rejected we imagine that only blowing up airport waiting-rooms or taking whole cruise ships hostage, or exploding airplanes filled with students will be loud enough acts to make us heard. The consequences to society of unlived imagination are terrifying.

Our inability to house fantasy may lead to an opposite kind of madness, now not of falling into the gap and being swept away by our images, but a wild fear of their pulling us so far away from a sense of reality that we dismiss every act of imagination as empty fantasy, patently mad. Our images do not express our experience to us, do not form a prelude to real living, but pull away from life, taking much of our energy with them. We withdraw from life. We just do not have the energy to dare, the zest to join in, whether at work, in outings, worship, or our own reveries. Everything fades, goes limp. Instead of our consciousness finding support, like a circulating life-blood, from our imagining, the blood drains away.[11] We are left only with a bedraggled self-consciousness, an awkward tentativeness, or worse, a kind of alert scanning-ray consciousness looking to repel anyone who comes too close.[12] A large piece of our capacity to live splits away from full functioning. Our energy is not lost or even repressed so much as dissociated; it seems to exist in another room, a secret place shut off from us by a strong padded door. Thus others cannot freely participate in our life either. Living becomes a melancholy unshared plodding through the day.

When we reject the resources of the imagination, refusing to receive, to look at, and reflect on the images that come to us, we do great harm to our outer social being and perhaps even more to our inner psychic being. Theological questions arise: Are there such things as false images? Can we be misled by the evil imaginings of our hearts as the Psalmist puts it? Were the old spiritual directors right in telling us to get rid of all imaginings if we would learn to pray?

Another way to pose this set of questions, in large abstract terms, is to ask if something can be psychologically true if it is theologically false. The answer, it is clear, must be No. Psyche and soul hang together, belong to the same person. We are not hybrids or trees with grafted parts. We grow our way forward, all of a piece. Our development continues until death involves all of our parts.

To put the point even more strongly, all images are true if they belong to us, if they are truly ours. That characterizes the wide-open psyche. Even images which psychology might call distorted, mad, or pathological may reveal where a lost bit of our true self may be lurking. If we moralize instead of extending our hand to this mute orphaned bit of ourselves, the missing part can come to us only through repetitive compulsion, or a perverse sexuality.[13] We shut the door instead of opening it so that this split-off part can come in and find its own place joining the rest of us. On the other hand, blind acquiescence is no good either. A self-indulgent or sentimental ignoring of what such compulsion or perverse images may do to us or to others can be very costly. Quantities of wasted time here may add up to a wasted life. That is at least as bad as moralizing.[14]

Letting images be there, seeing what they are, and reflecting on them means we are moving deliberately to the encounter. Ego and image meet, mix, confront. Two worldviews face each other, that of our conscious ego and the values of our culture contained in it, and that of the unconscious, with its crude, raw power expressed in images that fascinate, pull, push, arouse, draw us on.

We need to ask what it is that holds our attention in a pornographic-magazine picture of a woman, lacquered, airbrushed, reduced to an array of parts, all surfaces. What catches us? Is it the dismantling of the power image of Woman, no longer a person here, let alone a power, but merely a big breast, a hairy pubis? Do we now control her?[15] Are we rescued from feeling controlled by the female? What is it about a man's sexual potency and performance, openly suggested in slick ads, that arouses interest? Does the confinement in a shining photographic frame compensate for feeling under the thumb of men in a culture, and such dimensionless men at that? Do we find relief from major anxieties about our own sexuality, our own power in reducing persons to parts? Is that part-object way of proceeding involved in the resurgence of interest in the figure of the goddess? For here again woman is relieved from being a whole person and instead finds power in being identified with fertility, blood milk, a reproductive sexuality.

We are led into further theological questions. Why do we turn away from this sort of inquiry? Why do we reject what our imagination offers? Why do we turn away so quickly from the good, for that is indeed what we are doing, rejecting what God offers? These ancient questions gain freshness when approached through the psyche in the healing work of the imagination. We must look again at the possibility of wholeness, at the enterprise of growth. We need, with whatever difficulty, to let be the thoughts and pictures that come to us around our visions of the good, of wholeness, of peace, all our images of the good. We need to see what actually is there. If we do, we will have to acknowledge that we feel anxiety about the good, that we even dread it.[16] What could this mean?

There is a whole world of things caught up here, large and small. On the small side, we can learn from child analysts that seriously ill children refuse to play because of the fearful fantasies that they know will be let loose in their games. Treatment with such children amounts to imaginative playing, even if fearful and fantastic.[17] The therapy room becomes a safe enough place for the inner world of a child. The therapist is assigned different parts of that inner world, playing a witch, a naughty baby who must be beaten, a mother who eats up her children. The child comes to feel safe enough to let the images be, to see them, to play them out. Such imagining is the work of healing. Without it, a child stays mute, remote, unable to enter into life. For fear of the archetypal power of the images, the child does not pick up the toy.

Similarly, for fear of the sheer power and energy connected

with our adult imaginings, we may refuse to let our images be, to see them, to hold them, to reflect upon them. What happens to us, as child or adult, as the result of such refusal, is that we do not grow adequate defenses to manage all this psychic energy, do not learn how to hold it, put it aside, or use it when we really need it. Instead, we resort to magic means of control. A crucial example is when a child is not given time to learn, slowly, bit by bit, control of its bowel movements. That central life-process involves early fantasizing about the movements as a way of getting rid of persecuting inner elements which threaten a child. Undealt with, they may continue to menace, as they did Martin Luther, who advises us to discharge the devil from our bowels, or to discharge upon Satan. The unliberated, unimagining child suffers not only constipation or diarrhea but also must endure not being able to use its bowels as part of its personal way of being, enjoying the pleasure of moving them. They remain alien, something not altogether trustworthy, not really owned. Magic now means to control bowel movements through laxatives or coagulators, to use substitutes for real bowel ease, never to have them for one's own.

On a psychic level the personality feels victimized by its accumulated fears and threats, and resorts to magic to expel them. That again usually means projecting them onto one's neighbor. Not me, thee. Not us, them. Get rid of the thee's and them's and the world will be safe. What a short distance it may be from learning to play with the images that surround bodily functions to peace negotiations that affect world populations. When we do not find or create our own personal ways of handling aggression, we try to imitate someone else's way, someone we have magically gobbled up, thinking we can just appropriate their being. We are stuck then with the truly alien, the synthetic. We feel cheated even though we have done the stealing. Feeling cheated, we come to suspect the single or multiple other of persecuting us and easily enough we can then arrange to bring about such persecution by others. It is an incomparable way to avoid facing or even knowing how we have failed ourselves by a failure of imagination.

If we really give and take one from the other, we are really fed, each by the other, and we can grow our own way of being imaginative, or aggressive, or mathematical, or of speaking a language or riding a horse or preaching a sermon. The other does not sit in us, large and lumpy, like undigested food. Witches, remember, always gulp down people, food, whatever, in great unassimilated lumps which sit in them like stones.[18] As a result witches are always hungry. Then voracious appetite skips over the work of digestion, which psychically is a form of contemplation in which we make things our own. Hence, witches never get enough, always feel cheated, persecuted, and vengeful toward all those persecutory others. The magic introjection of the other in an effort to control can only issue in envy and a life of endless struggle.[19] Magic is no substitute for real defenses, which are flexible, which put energies within our reach, and protect us from their negative powers.

We need protection as well as channels for the great forces that primordial images present to us. Archetypal images are galvanizing. They compel us to identify with them instead of doing the work of trying to understand them. Rather than receiving and containing the images and sorting them through, we are in constant danger of simply becoming the images. Theologically, this is a refusal to incarnate and breeds idolatry instead. The young know this as they feel spurts of seemingly boundless physical energy well up in them and enlargements of emotional capacity. They often try to become the ideal image of themselves, to enact and fall right into the greater personality they look to be. The reality of time, the limits even of their great energy, the need for sleep and regeneration of strength, will force changes in their heroic image of themselves as able to do all sports, get top grades, conduct a full-sized social life, stay up all hours. Depression usually follows, with the realization that they must choose, perhaps only one or two things. They learn to relate to their image, not to try to become it.

Modern drama, from Ibsen and Strindberg to the Theater of the Absurd, is filled with examples of those who have identified with their images, who have acted out their fantasies, without recognizing what they were doing. The consequences range from the pitiful to the tragic. In Ibsen, reformers and idolators, such as the overdetermined reformer Gregers Werle in *The Wild Duck* and the compulsive pursuer of perfection Hilde Wangel in *The Master Builder*, assert "the claim of the ideal," destroy families and lead innocent people to their deaths. They never face the fact that they are utterly identified with their fantasies, and are quite content to let others be victimized by them.[20] In Strindberg, the enactments of identification become more complex. Men and women, driven far beyond the social niceties or the rule of family protocol by their enraged sexuality, are almost always just on the verge of standing aside to see what it is of the male in the female or the female in the male that makes sexual relationship so demanding, so bitter, so defeating for them. The demands of a husband and wife and daughter in *The Father* lead to the possibility of self-examination. The bitterness that the defeats engender turn self-examination into arraignment of the other. What looked like the possibility of understanding how much a man and a woman may mirror each the other's sexuality turns violent: two straitjackets are required, one psychological, the other physical. Desire gone sour choreographs *The Dance of Death*, Strindberg's two-part masterpiece, in which a stroke, following a sword dance, does in one of the two major characters, leaving the other celebrating "The wonderful peace of death." But neither figure ever realizes that they have identified with their sexual images and acted them out; all they know is the consequences of so doing. Only in the trilogy *To Damascus*, where all the characters are mirror images of each other and ultimately different sides of the central figure, called The Stranger, is there any recognition on the part of the characters that their failure to deal consciously with their imagination and to admit the extent to which they are living their fantasies has led to identification, idolatry, and despair where there should have been reconciliation, healing, and hope.

Strindberg's allegorical names for the forms of the pervasive consciousness and catapulting unconscious of his trilogy—The Lady, The Mother, The Beggar, The Confessor, The Madman, The Tempter, etc.—catch much of what gives such lasting strength to the plays of Pirandello and Chekhov, Beckett, Ionesco, and Stoppard. Their variously bemused and befuddled figures are strangers to themselves at least as much as they are to each other.[21] Chekhov's turn-of-the-century Russians make their jokes, pull their long conversational faces, play at the appointed games of an embattled bourgeoisie, not to tell us or themselves that the revolution is coming, but to confess that their fantasies about moving to Moscow, reforesting Russia, in *The Three Sisters*, or snatching up the family orchard before its beauties are turned into the dead soil of a housing development, and reawakening youthful fervor in aging bodies, in *The Cherry Orchard*, just won't do. There is a missing reality, a true sense of purpose, that neither dream idylls in the one case nor the possibility of social reform in the other will bring.[22]

Pirandello offers a way out—or rather more deeply in. It is all a dream. It is all theater. Pick your part. Learn it well. Know it is a part in the dream drama to which we are all fated, and all shall be well, or if not well, then at least amusing. Like the title character in *Henry IV* who insists he is the eleventh-century Holy Roman Emperor, sometimes out of madness, sometimes playing at madness, let us take advantage of the accidents of life, such as being thrown from a horse and losing one's memory. If events really produce an amnesia in which the unconscious casts us in such a fine gaudy role as the medieval monarch, so much the better. We can indulge our richest fantasies and most vindictive, parade in the raiment of power and attack, hire people to make up a court, even kill our enemies, real or fancied, and know we will be protected by the freedom from judgment conferred by amnesia, as the man playing at being Henry IV is protected—for life. If the gods have not been good enough to provide us with a fall from a horse, there are endless other opportunities to be knocked on the head. Things are what you make them to be, says Pirandello, which is as good a translation of *Cosi è (s'e vi pare)* as any of the others that have been tried to render the name of that beguiling drama of misplaced identities and loyalties. Just be sure, as the fables of actors and authors and directors of Pirandello insist, that you know what you are doing. Choose, as the odd-lot personages of *Six Characters in Search of an Author* and *Tonight We Improvise* must do, to wear or not to wear your theatrical mask. Do not simply fall into it, half-conscious or unconscious as, for example, so many of the miserable unfulfilled people in Eugene O'Neill's dramas do.[23]

That is the great force that Beckett and Ionesco unleashed and that Harold Pinter and Tom Stoppard and Edward Albee were caught up in, a theater of choice and indeterminacy, in which the grand Pirandellian option of a sumptuous dream freely entered almost always loses out to the destructive winds of chance. It does not matter, ultimately, whether the vaudevillian tramps of *Waiting for Godot* are being stood up by the deity or their own mad hopes. The dream sustains. Like the flophouse dramaturgy of *Endgame* or the fragmentary exchanges between the title figures in *Krapp's Last Tape*—the white-faced, purple-nosed, near-sighted, half-deaf Krapp and his tape recorder—the hope is in the open dream. It is a hope based in the theology of the absurd. Against all the evidence, Beckett's corroded old codgers wait, believing something, someone will turn up. The past, simply by being the past, guarantees a future. As for the present, that is a time for remembering the past and crafting a future from it. It is enough, little as it is, poor as their past has been, to create a bemused stubbornness in Beckett's decaying old people. In *Godot,* the tramps' trousers fall. They sit immobile in a tableau of arrested motion. They can only mime the futility of their years, the emptiness instinct in their reminiscences. "Perhaps my best years are gone," the Krapp of the tape-recorder says. "When there was a chance of happiness. But I wouldn't want them back. Not with the fire in me now. No, I wouldn't want them back." The fire in him? Just enough to hold him in place, "motionless staring before him," while the tape unwinds, without content, its only contribution a visual one, turning round for the eye to see.[24]

It is not a great richness of material that such characters bring back to their moments of self-inquiry, but self-inquiry is what they undertake. The distance between their reflections on their lives and the masters of the intellectual game who people Stoppard's *Jumpers* and *Travesties* is not that great. If anything, Beckett's bedraggled persons, simply by the nature of their bedragglement, are closer to measured thought. They are not easily stampeded into donning rhinoceros-heads, the symbolic apparatus by which Ionesco shows, in the play called *Rhinoceros*, how easily a country can be converted to senseless, self-defeating totalitarian ritual and belief. For rhinoceros heads, which everybody craves in a France occupied by a maddening fantasy, substitute the wearing of swastikas and the raising of the arm in stiff-boned salute to a Hitler—or a Stalin—or a Mussolini—or a Ceausescu. Ionesco, a Romanian who settled in France, was a survivor of several brands of rhinoceros-headedness, of occupying powers with which a population identified.[25]

In *Jumpers,* Stoppard's professional philosopher is shrewdly named George Moore, identifying him with a famous British thinker, G.E. Moore, though not equating the two. The imaginary Moore says, "Credibility is an expanding field. . . . Sheer disbelief hardly registers on the face before the head is nodding with all the wisdom of instant hindsight." It is a losing game. After more than two-thirds of his play has moved through its witty exercises, the Professor of Moral Philosophy can produce no better wisdom than this: "How does one know what it is one believes when it's so difficult to know what it is one knows." The ironic answer is left to *Jumpers'* all-purpose intellectual bureaucrat and university administrator, Sir Archibald Jumper: "Do not despair—many are happy much of the time; more eat than starve, more are healthy than sick, more curable than dying; not so many dying as dead; and one of the thieves was saved."

The fatuity with which most people meet the central events and dominating figures of their time is the burden of Stoppard's *Travesties*, a quick tour de farce through Zurich in the last year of the First World War. Lenin, James Joyce, and Tristan Tzara, the *éminence grise* of Dadaism, are all in residence. We meet them directly. We meet them through the faltering consciousness of Henry Carr, an only too plausible British consular official in Zurich. Carr can do little better with Tzara's elegant cynicism, as he accounts for his sitting out the war living "bravely in Switzerland" rather than dying "cravenly in France," than a noisy bluster: "My God, you little Rumanian wog—you bloody dago—you jumped-up phrase-making smart-alecy arty-intellectual Balkan turd!!!" For Joyce, with whom he has crossed swords over debts incurred in a production of Oscar Wilde, he has a dream: "dreamed I had him in the witness box, a masterly cross-examination, case practically won, admitted it all, the whole thing . . . and I *flung* at him—'And what did you do in the Great War?' 'I wrote *Ulysses,*' he said. 'What did you do?' " Carr comments: "Bloody nerve." But his memories of the time and the grand figures are warm: "Great days . . . Zurich during the war. Refugees, spies, exiles, painters, poets, writers, radicals of all kinds. I knew them all. Used to argue far into the night. . . . I learned three things in Zurich during the war. I wrote them down. Firstly, you're either a revolutionary or you're not, and if you're not you might as well be an artist as anything else. Secondly, if you can't be an artist, you might as well be a revolutionary . . . I forget the third thing."[26]

Better, these lines tell us, a cackling dismissal, fitted out with phrases from a well-stocked bag of Yahoo tags and answers, than any sort of serious examination of one's experience, or that most strenuous and defeating kind of self-inspection, of oneself undergoing the experience. Better, the Absurdists and their progenitors, Ibsen, Strindberg, Chekhov, Pirandello, tell us, look at these rituals of dismissal and despair, inspect them closely. See how close or how far they come from the integrating measures of self-examination and self-realization which the characters involved keep promising to adopt. See how the holding of the imagination at bay becomes nothing less than a dread of integration, for that is the inevitable end when we identify with our images and act out our fantasies rather than bring them to full consciousness, as best we can, and look at them and know them for what they are.

We must face our dread of integration itself and its dwarfing of our heroic self-images and repudiation of the claims of magic. Sometimes we fear integration so much we organize madness to protect ourselves against it. A planned disintegration protects us from the terrible anxieties connected with the integrating process.[27] Integration means gathering and putting the parts of ourselves and of our world together. It requires going out, sometimes, on long journeys into ourselves and out of them to look for the missing parts. That is why some people involve themselves in one kind of therapy after another, often for decades.

They are searching for the missing elements of self and world which will confirm that life lives whole and with grace in them. Without that pearl of great price all else is dross.

Putting together the disparate parts means feeling the anxieties of love next to the pressures of hate and knowing the dread that hate can destroy love. It means allowing ourselves to acknowledge that our dearest love may harbor an attraction to that opposite feeling and that our goal of independence may simply hide a fear of dependence, that our goal of mastery and willingness to strategize and pursue against all odds may conceal a helplessness in the face of others, where we are doomed to wait always for their actions or reactions. We discover that someone we thought we hated we actually sympathize with, or worse, would like to be. We find that the person we run from in life turns up in our dreams as someone ridiculously attractive sexually.

Being integrated means carrying conflict and suffering wherever they may lead. "Probably the greatest suffering in the human world," says Winnicott, "is the suffering of normal or healthy or mature persons."[28] We must tolerate our ambivalences and accept full responsibility for all of our feelings, worthy and unworthy alike. No more can we indulge the luxury of blaming other people, our parents, our lost loves, those who abused us, an environment that failed us, our terrible time in history, war, illness, or our refugee status. Integration means accepting all our experience, claiming all of it as our own, to make use of, to live with and to live from, to suffer.

We feel sadness at the moral ambiguity of our world, of ourselves, of all those we know. We feel sorrow at the human plight. We can allow ourselves to feel dangerously vulnerable to others' pain. So be it. That is the way of psyche and soul. That is the open, honest, healing way of prayer. If we go on praying over the years, our ability to numb ourselves to others' lives, with all their predicaments and suffering relentlessly diminishes, until it altogether disappears. We become porous to others and vulnerable to their wounds.

Integration means awareness of all these issues and dangers. It is not a blotting out, but a letting be of what is there, a seeing of reality, a dealing with it. Integration means linking memories to form a continuous line of past, present, and future, a thread of personal life that obliterates the dimension of time as it welcomes it. We do not break it but endure its breakings when trauma and agony temporarily interrupt our being. Integration means gathering up the broken bits of life where we have felt mad, and being willing to be aware of that bit of madness in us.

Finally, "Integration brings with it an expectation of attack."[29] Pulling together into a Me, as Winnicott puts it, amounts to repudiation of all the Not-me world around us. Further, when we first come together into a self, the world external to ourselves is more clearly defined than ever before and we may feel more exposed and vulnerable as a result, even become paranoid. Theologically, one thinks of Jesus's experience of evil. Right after baptism and acknowledgment from heaven of his sonship, the same Spirit that had so encouraged him drives him into exposure to tempting voices in the desert. Indeed, even his birth excites such envy and fear in King Herod that he orders all newborn sons slaughtered. Choruses of thanksgiving for the birth of the savior are made harsh and strained by the crying of mothers and fathers who can not be consoled at the murder of their infants. We learn that from birth the coming of the good is marked by the outbreak of evil. Liturgically, the slaughter of the innocents follows only three days after the celebration of the nativity. Jesus loses his innocence when he is just three days old.

Jesus, a remarkably whole person, saw and knew evil as attacking him, from the time of birth to the cross. When we pull ourselves together into something like an integrated whole, we also will know attack and must be aware of it so that we can set aside the defensive acts within ourselves to make our attack into a defense of wholeness rather than a mere personal impulse that threatens our own and everyone else's chance of integration.

What we defend when we defend wholeness is the living-place of our defining spirit, the place where our imagination feels at home and we can feel safe from madness, from depression, despair, and a life of impossible fragmentariness. The role of the imagination in this move toward integration is not to hinder the spiritual life but to make it possible. It is to make us feel at home, all of us, in and with all our parts. It is to permit us to do what the masters of the modern theater show their central characters doing—doing something and knowing that they do it, or at the very least hoping to know. It is to permit us that meeting of psyche and soul where when we have an experience we can see ourselves having the experience, can participate in it and, when necessary, stand apart from it at the same time. It is to make us not only know ourselves but claim ourselves. We are no longer in exile from ourselves, alien to our own being. We have come home.

Chapter 4

Imagination and Ministry

Preaching is a strange business, and preparing people to preach, or for any of the works of ministry, teaching, counseling, whatever, is stranger still. We lead lambs to slaughter: training them how to get up each week in public and speak about the Holy, in a sermon, a Bible-study class, or in counseling or spiritual direction. We are training people to go into the dark. The work of ministry goes on in the trenches, and nowhere more so than in the brief—and we always hope it will be brief—sermon.

A sermon, a talk, a word that counts, that is the assignment. Once a week, week after week, year after year, decade after decade, a lone soul must stand up publicly and speak about what comes like fire and burns us up, the Holy that summons us to leave our familiar country and journey into the unknown toward a whole new departure-point in everything we do, and merely on the basis of a promise. The Holy bids us identify with strangers across the world who suffer with pain much the same as ours even if it sometimes becomes more dramatic. This is our brother who is shot down in Vietnam, our husband who is being held hostage in Lebanon, our sister who cannot feed her starving child in famine-ridden Ethiopia. The odd presence we call the Holy can fold its skirts and disappear into the dark or just as easily into the blinding light, sometimes for years, so that we feel no answering presence in our prayers, our needs, our sufferings, see no signs, know no quickening of faith. Training people to do the work of ministry is like training them to go out absolutely alone again and again to the end of a very high diving board and over and over again to plunge into the deep waters below. Such a task needs every kind of psychological, spiritual, and aesthetic energy to sustain itself. It demands the healing work of the imagination just to get out there, let alone reach others.

Again we meet the gap. In teaching or counseling or spiritual direction the clergy must make room for all the pet gods people bring with them and for the images of God offered by scripture and tradition. We must confront head on the gap between these two types of images, often a frighteningly wide one. The clergy's work centers on imaginative linking across the gap. A sermon is such a linking, a drawing of lines of connection, where one must neither foist a private god-image on a congregation, nor impose a public image on the privacy of individual souls.[1]

In the first, we may become another Jim Jones insisting on our own god-image, demanding it be seen as God and we as God's messenger. If we coerce others into this way, it is usually because unconsciously we are ourselves coerced by falling into identification with a powerful god-image. An archaic image may possess our soul and make us strive to possess others' souls, even at the risk of their lives. Terrorism preaches on its texts this way. It demonstrates the extremes of madness to which we can come when our imagination cannot span the gap and must choose one side or the other, even violently. That is not so different from certain kinds of political preaching where the preacher urges a literal-minded kind of action following from the sermon. There is no room to sort out meanings, to make personal judgments, just hectoring from the pulpit with an implied threat that if the hearers do not execute the prescribed action, they must fail themselves and their faith.

In the contrary danger, so much fear exists in the preacher about the power of images that they must be excluded altogether. The preacher preaches a dry sermon, a technical exegesis, a sociological or historical or literary analysis of the times and places of the text, unrelated to the life of the people in the pews.[2] Or we get the biblical message in prepackaged form, a sanitized version handed down by authority—church, midrash, pope, bishop. No room is left to link the personal to the shared god-images. Nothing is spoken to the heart, to the soul, to the psyche. We hear a lot of words, but no Living Word. If preaching ignores the unconscious energies symbolized in our private images, our pet gods, those condemned to listen can only wait out the sermon politely, sometimes sleeping, more often donning the mask of attentiveness while behind it they plan menus, review the week, worry through a problem. A congregation comes hungry for the word, some connecting link between this world and the unseen one where faith resides. Too often it must go away hungry, disappointed, sad.

It is urgent that we pay attention to the private pictures of God that people bring with them. The pictures may be conscious, or unconscious, but they are always there, crafted from experiences that mark us deeply because they come from deep inside us and all around us. Though we may not understand the pictures, we do not forget them. They form themselves at every stage of our lives. A little boy, for example, saw God as Horse. In his drawing, the mane, forelock, and ears of the horse went right off the top of the page, even as God exceeds all our boundary lines. A priest of twenty years' standing was startled, humbled, made to laugh out loud when the eucharistic God suddenly appeared to him as Big Mama, a fat, contented black woman sitting at the center of creation in her swivel chair, tuning in different parts of the world on her television set. An ex-nun, sorrowful still that in all her years in the convent she had never realized the personal relationship with God that she longed for and that she had been taught was available, is caught now by an impersonal image of God as a huge diamond of which she is one facet.

Our pet gods may be group gods, pictures we share in common with others of our same tribe. They may be images that speak of our experiences together as persons of the same race or creed, sex or color, geographical area or political belief. Recent theologies have insisted on these group god-images—God as black, female, gay, as oppressed, as psychic force. These are images that come out of particular lived situations that differentiate a personal from an abstract God. They speak of people's yearnings, needs, and perceptions of where mercy may be found. No preaching can have force that does not take account of these group gods. But equally, no preaching can long be effective that insists that every group take one group's god-image as the only true one. Either way we miss hearing about the God who stands over the gap, reaching for both oppressor and oppressed, gathering in white, yellow, and black, female and male. We do not hear about the wounded God, the redeeming God, when we hear only about the preacher's wounds or the preacher's version of the world's wounds. That may be interesting, even moving, but it is not the food of God that feeds multitudes. It can only leave us empty.

The pictures of God given in scripture and by tradition are far-ranging, startling, even violent. God in Samuel is a punisher of false priests who are careless with their vows. God cuts them off and breaks the priestly succession. God is a military commander sending Israel into battle or a mysterious presence that hovers over the mercy seat set above the ark in the center of the tent of the Holy of Holies. God is a high tower, a doorway, the one who sees our fear when our daughter is sick, the one who weeps when our brother dies. God comes as one who breaks the rules, relativizing them, knocking them out from under us as a prop we constantly misuse to defend us against the immediate experience of the religious imagination.[3]

By tradition, God comes to us as the One who nurses our beginnings as in John of the Cross, as the One who awaits our entrance into the central rooms of our Interior Castle, as in Teresa of Avila, as the One mysteriously born in our souls, as in Meister Eckhart, a winecask, as in Catherine of Siena, or as a Trinity of gemstone, fire, and word, as in Hildegard of Bingen, as the abyss of omnipotence, working on the soul with a relentless love that is "terrible and implacable, devouring and burning without regard for anything," as in Hadewijch of Brabant.[4] The task for each soul, and for the clergy as guardians of soul, is always to ask, to ponder, and imaginatively to weave connections across the gap between the two kinds of images, the personal and the traditional.

No preaching—or counseling or direction—can reach very far that does not take into account our unconscious and highly idiosyncratic images for God. These personal icons are created by our psyches out of the stuff of what we take in at the center of our being and then put out into the world, our introjections and projections.[5] These private god-images accompany us unbidden to every worship service, every class about religion, every effort to confront our own depths and to bring ourselves into prayer, every attempt to run away from religious faith or to practice it. That is why the work of chaplains in hospitals, prisons, schools, armies can be so gripping. People want a chaplain usually when they are in crisis. That is the time these odd pet gods jump forward, to help sustain us or to break under the strain of crisis. Right there, before a seeing chaplain's eyes, is a person's immediate, raw, untutored experience of God, able to be touched, spoken, communicated with, and linked up to wider, deeper resources of being and thus of faith.

This is a delicate moment, this meeting of the traditional resources of religion and of personal experience. On such a moment may hang the future of a person's religious life and access to that dimension of the spirit that defines an identity and gives it purpose in life. One man told of his father's loss of faith when he was six years old. A rabbi said to his class, God created the world. When the little boy raised his hand to ask, And who created God? the rabbi sharply smacked his knuckles with a ruler. A woman said she was expelled from Sunday School for asking questions such as, Were Adam and Eve cavemen? All she remembered of her religious instruction was being sent from the room to sit on the stairs outside the classroom, in disgrace.

A gap too often exists, between a teacher's or preacher's personal grasp and style of presenting the material of faith and a student's or parishioner's way of taking it and making it his or her own. Too much reliance on what everybody is supposed to know coerces the teacher to force material into a student's mouth, without allowing for personal habits and peculiarities of timing and tasting. Imposition will not do. This is not an occasion for surgical implants. A real touching of the unknown must take place. All the instruction can be correct and still the soul flees for its life.

Obviously, the opposite extreme will not work either. Exclusive reliance on the personal styles of the instructed, the listener, the communicant, is no better than the instructor, the preacher, the priest reducing everything to comfy little autobiographical bits. Providing nothing of the food of the tradition conveys a demand to the recipients to construct faith entirely out of scraps of personal experience. The recipient is starved for lack of real substance. In the miracle of the loaves and the fishes Jesus first blessed the bread and fish and gave thanks to God for them; only then did the food mysteriously multiply to feed thousands. To ask parishioners to create a whole meal out of the scraps they bring with them is to forget that God is the ultimate abundant source. We cannot provide all we need ourselves; if we could we would not be there.

Only imagination is delicate and tough enough to touch and yoke together the two sides in the exquisite task of religious education, which is after all for the formation and endurance of our souls. Here, for once, that spacious phrase "preparation for life" is appropriate. In psychological language, we are talking about the space between self and other, between God as our subjective-object and God as the objective-object.[6] Psychologically, a subjective-object is an other who reflects me, who functions in respect to me, for my needs, desires, and dependencies. A mother exists to feed, bathe, hold, and answer her infant; she does not exist in an infant's eyes separately, in her own subjective center of being. Mothers often complain that they are not allowed time off even for the bathroom, and the struggle of adolescence for a parent often consists in emerging from the status of self-object to becoming a person in one's own right. An objective-object exists outside my needs, desires, and dependencies. It finds its own frame of reference and may or may not be related to us quite independently of our wishes. It defies our omnipotence, or our illusory version of it.

Theologically, God as subjective-object is my picture of God, or our group's picture of God which reflects back to us our wishes, needs, and desires. This God does not exist apart from us, but is alive in our psychic life, in our shared rituals, celebrations, and mournings. The subjective God lives all bound up in and through our experiences, our projections, our introjections. We experience this God in intimacy—the God we talk to, rage against, bring our troubles to. This God helps keep us in being and constantly figures in our imaginative dialogue, whether positive or negative. For example, we may envision God as a stern, scowling rule-maker, always checking up on us, tallying our sins or, on rare occasion, our progress. What invariably gets reflected back to us is our inadequate performance, our falling short. Thus the ego that is kept in being is a wobbly one, fretful, worrying, always full of anxiety. In its tremulous state it may press the body toward high blood pressure, hypertension, ulcers, even a heart attack. On the other hand, this subjective-object God may stand as silent witness to our truest self, grounding us securely against the fitful currents of our worries and problems, passing fads in religion, all the threatening collectivities of our modern world.

Some of us simply forget about this subjective God. We formed a picture when young, modelled after father or mother, or even some benevolent beast or strong natural force, and then just put it aside, preoccupied with other kinds of growing. In crisis this old picture pops up again, to be used or to break under the strain of illness, death, divorce, loss of job, or comparable anxiety. Some of us continue throughout our lives to be preoccupied with this subjective-object God. We consult it, we revise it. With luck it continues to function as an active force promoting our integration.

Let it be stressed that we are talking as much of integration of the psyche as of the spirit. For often our god-images present us with left-out bits of ourselves that insist on being claimed. So the man who dreams of hearing Christ scream in agony on the cross, swearing and cursing at the suffering inflicted on him, is also being told about his own unclaimed suffering and his own unvoiced anger about it.[7] The subjective god-image bears toward our consciousness feelings, attitudes, impulses, angers, despairs, hopes, and unlived loves that we must attend to and integrate. The resurgence of the god-image in the form of the goddess points, for example, to a collective hunger for the missing feminine in ourselves, in our dealings with each other, in our treatment of the earth we live in.[8]

Theologically, God as objective-object is the God we hear about, are told about, read about, find discussed, argued over, and researched in religious studies. This is not the God of immediate experience, but a God that exists outside us and over against us. This God exists, regardless of our projections or our beliefs. He is not created by us nor does he exist just for us. This is the God held up to us traditionally as the "real" God, not the one made up out of our wishes. For God as an objective-object presents himself as social object, too, something we hold in common, devise rituals around, and find in sacred texts. This objective-object God is often presented as valid in a way that a subjective-object God cannot be, as somehow outside and therefore better than our "selfish" needs or desires. The fallacy of that view derives from the assumption that quantity means superiority, that the large-scale group ego transcends the personal ego with its small-scale wishes, needs, desires, and defenses. In fact, the personal ego-concerns just increase. Transcendence of that level of the ego does not proceed from a multiplication of egos. A social God does not necessarily possess less selfish projections than an individual god-image. Transcendence means coming or going outside the ego, beyond it, from or to a different level. Nonetheless, the objective-object God bears in upon us the fact that all through tradition generations of people have recognized the *that*ness and *what*ness of God that exist beyond the *this*ness of our private fashionings.[9]

Imagination, as it works in preaching and teaching, spiritual direction and counseling, shows us how to work in the gap between subjective and objective god-images and how to link them up so that we neither run the risk of idolatry on the one side nor a punitive superego attack on the other. One of the salutary virtues of church music is that it avoids these extremes —at least in theory—in its conversion of images into sound. The chorale preludes of German composers from Sweelinck to Buxtehude and Bach are handsome cases in point. These organ works were written, or improvised, to fix hymn tunes in the minds of their hearers, or more frequently, with the understanding that the tunes were highly familiar to the congregation and therefore any variations that were developed could be assured of a firm grounding in the listeners' ears and their supporting memories. It was the same sort of certainty that Mozart could have in writing variations on the tune we know as "Twinkle, Twinkle, Little Star," and that two centuries later Dohnanyi would depend on, using the same air for his *Variations on a Nursery Theme.*

How much of the subjective would a Buxtehude or a Bach allow to enter his church music? And if the subjective was kept under wraps, to the extent that genius permits, in the execution of what were in effect hymn-tune duties, what about the writing of Passions, of Masses, of all or large parts of a service? Zealous liturgists have long attacked the use, say, of a Mozart or Schubert setting of the mass in church, not to find fault with the music, but to keep it from bringing what they considered the noxious presence of self-expression into the clean air of communal devotions. The French make some move toward a solution in the place they give to organ improvisation or set organ pieces in the body of the mass, musically substantial, but as carefully molded to the sacred duty as possible. After the mass, an organ recital, from ten minutes to a half hour or more, permits the virtuosi to make their devotions without fear of exceeding the bounds of liturgical good taste, and virtuosi they are in the great French churches. Theirs is a succession of masters that includes César Franck, Widor, and Vierne, Dupré, Langlais, Tournemire, and Messiaen, and points directly at the vexed issue.[10]

Quite apart from differences of theological emphasis as they are reflected in church architecture, the absence or presence of paintings and statues, and the large-scale devotional works composed by Bach, Haydn, Schubert, Beethoven, Berlioz, Brahms, Stravinsky, Vaughan Williams, and the like, are we willing to ban from church any exercise of the imagination that does not fall comfortably into official definition of what is permissible? No Stravinsky Mass, no Poulenc *Stabat Mater,* no Verdi *Requiem?* No Matisse, Picasso, Léger, Bazaine? Must we wait until they have become so much a part of our tradition that we can worship in their midst as we do in churches designed by Christopher Wren or Michelangelo or Bernini, sitting under a Titian painting or a Masaccio fresco? Are the great works of sacred music to be reserved for occasions of great splendor when, as in the weeks of summer festival in the German-speaking countries, it is possible to cram a symphony orchestra into an organ loft and fit it out with appropriate soloists and conductor and worship the Lord with the aid of some of his most joyous votaries?

Our answer to these questions is a guarded one. The imagination is surely not to be banished from church, even if it sometimes proves to be a distraction. Churchgoing has more serious distractions today than Bach or Stravinsky, Picasso or Messiaen. When the great presence of the imagination of such figures leads to idolatry, then selective choice among their works is not simply indicated; it is commanded.

Idolatry can strike at the heart of our life in the church, in a sermon, in counseling or spiritual direction, even in a class discussion when persons speaking the words or giving the counsel have fallen into identification with their own or their own group's god-images, as a painter or a sculptor may do. An idol rears up in such identification. Every energy of soul and passion for the infinite floods into these images, no matter how tiny they may be, inflating them to carry the All of Reality in their minuscule parts. Congregations are diminished. Students are pushed toward discipleship, moved to play a role, not encouraged to grow their own relation to the text. Sometimes seminary students who come to the thesis-writing stage of their degree fall into an idolatry of the thesis. It must be perfect. How could it be less with such a subject? All creative thought evaporates in anxiety about the imperfect nature of their religious ideas. They fall under the tyranny of trying to bring the idealized, utopian image of the thesis, now become a god, into being. This is to fall into the gap. What follows is the positive madness of procrastination, of self-flagellation, of obsessive preparation and endless research. If the thesis is to be god-like, to achieve its own perfection, then another line of research always beckons, still another argument to polish, yet another book to be mastered. The opposite side of perfection falls on the students. Self-judgments come thundering down on their heads. They find themselves not merely imperfect but meager, mediocre. Productive work comes to a standstill.

One student postponed her thesis writing for years, always putting husband, child, this problem, that task, before her own work. She idealized not only the paper she needed to produce, but the time and space needed in order to produce it. Everything else had to be in order before she could tackle the final draft. In conference with her teacher she said she felt inadequate because the thesis was "just me," meaning, of no use to anyone else. Her teacher said, No, I am waiting, and so is your subject. That night the student dreamt she and her advisor were meeting about her thesis. "A slight interruption occurs, so we both go away somewhere. When we return, I am on stage before a big audience. I think it rude of me to speak only to my teacher. So I speak to everyone about my thesis!" A dream becomes a prayer. The imagination has intervened.

In spiritual direction this idolatry shows itself when a director fixates on a certain method of prayer, whether or not it fits the soul of the person involved. It plagues counselors with special theories about therapy. A counselor's identification with a theory leaves those being counseled with no choice. They must comply or reject the whole procedure. What is needed is a major shift toward imaginative identification with the other, with the client's point of departure. What does the world look like from that point of view? Where do openings present themselves? Where do the blocks come from? What is the real confusion? What is being defended against? Theory and good training are only the beginning in direction and counseling. Without the imagination, theory falls like a golden calf on the soul's intimations of God and the psyche's spontaneous gestures.

In our idolatries, we seek the perfect solution or solutions, the unanswerable thesis, the winning sermon, with none of the mess of ordinary life. We deny much, aggression especially. Winnicott, in response to questions put to him by a group of young Anglican priests on how to tell if they could help someone who came to them and when to refer such a person for psychiatric treatment, said, "If a person comes and talks to you and, listening to him, you feel he is *boring* you, then he is sick, and needs psychiatric treatment. But if he sustains your interest, no matter how grave his distress or conflict, then you can help him all right."[11]

We are more responsible for being boring than most of us would like to admit. To be boring is to strike at life, to prevent anything from happening, to kill imagination. The bore denies inner psychic reality and especially any instinctive impulse of desire or aggression. It is an anti-life defense that really bores us as we work to fix things in place instead of letting them flow, giving the psyche its right to go where it might, allowing feelings to gather. Boring others makes contact with them inauthentic. It may look like polite and proper communication, but it is not; it is coercive control.

The opposite way of falling into the gap in these areas—preaching, teaching, counseling, spiritual direction—does not arise from idolatrous identification with one's god-images, but from fear of images altogether. Here we substitute for the rules. We bundle up prepackaged definitions of who God is and hand them out, to ourselves, to our clients or parishioners. This is what to believe. Over and out. It is an opposite way to the first and yet the same. Both issue in the same coerciveness. Boredom, for example, is one of the principal ways preachers and teachers vent aggression against their hearers. We all know the drill: a slow-paced monotonous delivery, repetitious ideas, an endless dwelling on the terms of an assignment, a neat, precise, numerically identified, and endlessly dull spelling out of the text, ancient notes read verbatim for the thousandth time. The believer is driven mad. What a dangerous profession religion is! Think of Judgment Day when God asks, What did you do with my consuming fire? Just so much smoke, and so deadly dull!

If these ways of venting aggression against believers are not fully successful, we can always resort to stirring up persecutory anxiety. We give the right interpretation. If student or client balks, they cast themselves out of the circle of belief. The correct method of prayer is laid before you. If your experience does not conform, clearly you are a great distance from God. You may even be damned. The correct social analysis is delivered in the classroom. You do not concur? Clearly you are guilty of all the social sins against your neighbors. You are sexist, racist, Eurocentric, whatever fits. No space is given to find personal relation to the text. To do that we must take notice of how the images in the text actually strike us. Which repel? Which fascinate? Which speak to our psyche, to our soul?

An imaginative line of inquiry does not exclude any of the standard methods of interpretation. It will not turn away from history or literary form or linguistic reconstruction or whatever we may be able to discover about the habits of mind and expectations of those to whom the great texts were first brought. The imagination will not blanch, either, at being reminded of the biases and prejudices of the present day or of any part of the past. An attention to images and their psychic and spiritual resonances balks at nothing, but it does insist on the personal. What, we must ask, is their subjective effect upon us, and what in their objective existence, as part of the history and structure of symbols, will we find useful as a way of understanding their effect upon us. This is the hermeneutic of depth psychology.[12] What, we want to know, does the psyche contribute to the exegesis of a text in itself, in our reception of it? These images in the text are live symbols that address, summon, and even judge us. What is our response?

On the level of the objective existence of images, we might ask why are some images from the Hebrew Bible carried over into the New Testament—and beyond—and others discarded? By what means, theological, psychological, historical, or literary, can we discover why images were dropped or held onto? The symbol of "the land" persists. So does the "Son of man." God as military leader, as urging mass executions, implacable avenger, fades. On the subjective level, where these images affect actual people deeply and link exegesis to pastoral care, we need to ask why religious images take up residence in people at all, and so insistently, with such unbroken energy. Negative images can wound people for decades, such as the image of God hardening his heart against the Pharaoh or against a whole people like the Amalekites. People ask, Did God harden his heart against me when I got cancer? Does that account for the death camps? No use denying it: people ask these questions because the ancient images still pursue us. It is true of a positive religious image, too, of course. Both Martin Luther King, Jr.'s rhetoric of nonviolence and the Moral Majority's appeal to fundamentalist doctrine were rooted in spiritual imagery. Both recognized the possibilities for positive conversion of persecutory anxiety.

In spiritual direction and counseling, which we link together here because both are so concerned with the pace and style of individual growth, we can stir up an anxiety that feels persecutory by insisting on identifying the good images and the bad ones. These are right for the soul, those are wrong. Think that, feel that, see that, and your psyche and soul will bloom. As for the others, the bad ones, that way lies damnation—or neurosis, anyway.[13] Prescriptions crowd out the imagination. Once again, we are coerced and find we cannot comfortably receive and accept the pictures our psyche tosses up to us from the unconscious, or the winding ways of the soul our actual journey to God is meant to take. We can take counsel and example here from the work of artists, composers in particular, who have had so often to choose between imaginative extremes to achieve the integration which a successful work of art represents.

Integration is by definition a bringing together of diverse elements. It can be a task of a besetting complexity. It is never a simple matter, in which the elements to be brought together, often quarrelsome ones, just fall into place. But it is often an occasion for grace, never more so than in the work of a successful composer. The examples are many. The most persuasive for our purposes are those of the composers of sets of themes and variations, for here the vertebrate nature of the form demands an exercise in integration.

One set of examples, all working with the same theme, is particularly engaging. The theme is that of the twenty-fourth Caprice of the legendary violin virtuoso Niccolo Paganini. All of the Caprices, and not the least of them No. 24, are virtuoso display pieces designed to show off the abundant technique of a performer famous in the early nineteenth century for diabolic skills on his instrument. The theme of the twenty-fourth, itself subject to twelve variations, is beguiling, and a long list of musicians of very different tastes and temperaments, and almost none of them with virtuosic concern, has responded to its allures. There is Johannes Brahms to begin with, with two books of piano variations on the theme. His is a demanding work, a moving one, that does not turn away from technical display as it moves through two sets of fourteen variations, each to its fitting coda. There are complexities of rhythm, of interval, of hand-crossing, of little-finger pyrotechnics. But what one remembers of the work, unless one has been a pianist struggling with its finger-breaking demands, is its wit, its sweetness, its shifts from tender sentiment to brusque assertion, and all held together by a perfection of form.

After the Brahms, the next masterful use of the Caprice 24 theme is Rachmaninoff's in his *Rhapsody on a Theme of Paganini.* It holds second place only to his Second Piano Concerto in the loyalties of pianists and audiences. Its twenty-four variations move piano and orchestra through tunes and textures that suggest a collection of tales, romantic, robust, momentarily posturing, more often elegant. It never settles for either virtuosic or sentimental excess. Integration, a wholeness that is presented with fine sequential logic to the ear and the imagination, takes the *Rhapsody* well beyond soloist duty.

A half dozen years after the *Rhapsody,* in 1941, the Polish composer Witold Lutoslawski produced his set of *Variations* on the same theme, this time for two pianos. This is the most playful of the group, with some debts perhaps to both Brahms and Rachmaninoff, but with its own acerbic humor, a probing of the percussive nature of the piano which recalls Paganini's stretching of instrumental resources, and some measures of recollection here and there to remind the listener or performer how far-ranging the work of integration can be, even in so brief and bumptious a work.

Boris Blacher's *Orchestral Variations* on the Paganini theme in 1947 is a sober enough investigation by a provocative German modernist with a taste for a kind of philosophical reflection in music. One hears it in the Paganini *Variations*, but even more in the remarkable coupling of tenor voice and string quartet he effects in his setting of Wallace Stevens' *Thirteen Ways of Looking at a Blackbird.* These terse poetic rituals of the imagination make us see in sharp relief a blackbird against autumn winds, icicles, window glass, and snow. Blacher's integration of the thirteen poems, from two to six lines in length, is achieved by moving from the outside in. Like a Renaissance poet or an Ezra Pound playing with the maddening mathematics of the sestina form, Blacher connects the first and thirteenth poems, the second and twelfth, and so forth, until, in effect, he comes to the core of the music, the seventh. It may take several hearings for this structure to reveal itself; it may never be clear. It does not matter. The ceremonies of integration are not directed to an easy appreciation or a precise logic. Dedicated to wholeness, they require a wholeness in response, a movement of the person, like the soft, touching sounds of Blacher's music and Stevens' verse, that mixes head and heart, rational statement and irrational. It is a splendid example of moving across gaps and not falling into them, of a dedicated use of freedom of imagination to achieve wholeness.[14]

In the gap between the group's god-images and our own, between the official, the traditional, the scriptural and what our own imagination throws up to us, whole new worlds of experience await us. Behold, I do a new thing! God says. The new thing draws on both sides of the gap and consists of neither one nor the other exclusively nor even a deliberate, recognizable combination of the two. It is all of these and more. It is the imagination at the source. It is a new being in the service of integration.

Chapter 5

The People Who People Our Imagination

No book on the imagination can proceed without attention to the high place of sexuality within it. Even if we feel an oaf about spirituality, a dolt in our response to the creative imagination, a know-nothing about the unconscious, still we know the stirrings of sexual images and know them well. They tickle the base of our spine or make our lower back hot. Liquid sensations envelop our bellies, fiery feelings mount between our legs. Palms sweat, inhalations and exhalations quicken and make us feel about to swoon. Our bodies take over in motion and need, sweeping past our reticence, or any considerations of appropriateness. It takes so little, too. Sexual feelings can start from an unbidden fantasy, a picture in a book, a dream, a glance at or from a stranger, let alone the excited look or scent of a long-loved partner.

Sexual imaginings people our psyches with likely and unlikely others. They constitute the rock bottom of fantasy life that one way or another touches all of us and almost from the beginning. The intensity of sexual feelings in little children can still make their elders gasp. When a little child says, "When I get as big as Pop I'm going to marry you!" or "Give me one of those wet kisses you give to Daddy!" or "Oh Daddy, Daddy, I love you, I love you; Goodnight, Goodnight!" complete with entwining arms in a summer seersucker nightgown, we know we are up against passion. At the other end of life, there are many elderly men and women in whom the fires of sexuality have deepened to a constant presence, ready to ignite at the right moment, with the right imagining, and the right person.

Sexuality is not just a part of life, but rather a central way in which we put ourselves into life. It applies to us all, elderly or young, single, partnered, widowed, divorced, presexual, heterosexual, homosexual, lesbian. It does not need the exaggerations or distortions of pornography, the dislocations of gothic romance, or hardboiled mystery. In the literature of every culture and every time, in religious writing, sexual images stir our fantasy and people our imagination. We find ourselves caught by the most ridiculous or obscene scenarios, from the hilarious and the perverted to the most sublime. Mystics and even depth psychologists use the images of sexual embrace and penetration, of every sort of sexual meeting and concern, to rescue for our understanding the plunge into the unknown, the reach up into the spirit, into the blissful reception of an all-encompassing unity.[1]

It is hard to think of any writing more intensely sexual or more directed to a unifying fullness of experience than the following sets of lines of verse and prose:

> Open to me, my sister, my love,
>   my dove, my undefiled:
> For my head is full of dew,
>   and my locks of the drops of the night

> O love, so precipitate, so violent, so ardent, so impetuous, suffering the mind to entertain no thought but of thyself, spurning everything, despising everything which is not thyself, content with thyself alone! Thou disturbest all order, disregardest all usage, ignorest all measure. Thou dost triumph over in thyself and reduce to captivity whatever appears to belong to fittingness, to reason, to decorum, to prudence or counsel.

>   O sweet contest; of woes
> With loves, of tears with smiles disputing!
> O fair and friendly foes,
> Each other kissing and confuting!
> While rain and sunshine, cheeks and eyes
> Close in kind contrarities.

It is equally difficult to think of meditations more securely spiritual than the two sets that follow:

What was begun by the celestial will
You would have thought was bound to prosper
well,
But when I see the angry clouds that fill
The sky, and how Aeolus' winds are freed,
I think it was by ordinance of Hell
My shipwreck on this reef was long decreed.

So great is the good which is set before me that I live in hope of it without suffering; if I do not achieve it, I shall be so wretched that I shall have found Hell in this world. On the one hand, it gives me great happiness; on the other, my life is full of trials; it is placed in the scales with death, afraid that fear will frustrate my hope.

The first quotation is from The Song of Songs, chapter 5, verse 2. The second is from St. Bernard of Clairvaux's commentary on The Song of Songs, one of the last verses on which he commented, the third verse of the third chapter. He arrived at that point after twenty years of conferences on the Song with his monks. Almost all of his commentary shares a similar intensity of feeling and grace of style. The third is one stanza from "The Weeper," the seventeenth-century poet-priest Richard Crashaw's great extravagant baroque tribute to Mary Magdalene. The content in each case is spiritual; the rhetoric, sexual.

The last two sets of lines are from love poems. The first of the two is the concluding sextet of the twentieth sonnet of Louise Labé. The sixteenth-century poet is sometimes called *la belle cordière,* because her father and her husband were ropemakers, sometimes *la Sappho lyonnaise,* to point to her city of origin, Lyon, and the voluptuousness of her verses, not because of any other connection with the poet of Lesbos, for she probably knew no Greek and makes clear, as she opens her first elegy, that Phoebus Apollo gave her an instrument that used to sing of Lesbian amour but will now anguish for her kind of love. Hers, like the lover of the last poet, Ausias March, is defiantly heterosexual. March, a too-little known Catalan poet of the fifteenth century, is a master of the sexual imagination in verses that cry out as Labé's do at the torments of unrequited love but also celebrate moments of great favor from love's deity. The point is that the deity is in it. "The body is so united with the soul," Ausias March exclaims, "that no action in man can ever be called single. . . ." The result is often conflict, confusion, or a short-lived peace, "since suffering endures longer than pleasure." In the great long lament for his dead love, from which these last quotations come, the poet asks at the last to be united with his lady: "before my life ends, I wish my body to lie with its arms around hers. . . . On the Day of Judgment, when we take on flesh and bone, we shall share out our bodies without distinction." These two poets with the manner of ascetics are dealing with the matter of sexuality.

It is not at all difficult, with a small exercise of imagination, to see how men and women of such intense feelings must move from one end of the spirals of interiority to the other. The language of sexual intimacy is the only fitting way to give words to the experience of the unspeakable joy of that purification, illumination, and movement toward union that we call the mystic way. Equally, the longing must be for the most direct experience of the life of the spirit for those for whom the fires of sexuality have not been enough, no matter how great their own burning zeal, either because they have not been answered in kind or because their lover has been claimed by death. And so at last Ausias March can say in his verses, "I do not ask you to give me physical health or any goods of nature or fortune, but merely, God, to make me love you, for I am certain that the greatest good derives from this."[2]

There is no mistaking the impulse of mystics to use the highly colored sexual imagery of The Song of Songs as the best available rhetoric to describe their spiritual ardors or the all but inevitable move of the great sensualists toward the life of the spirit, whether out of disappointment with the life of the flesh or recognition that body and soul are most deeply intertwined when either is pursued to extremes. The connection is indissoluble. We find it in the East as well as the West. The Indian *Gita Govinda* and a whole literature of religiously directed eroticism closely parallels what we find in the Song and the writings of the masters of the spiritual life who have used its language or their own elaborate variations upon it.[3] Everywhere that the passions of the flesh claim articulate devotees, metaphors of the divine take their place, from the exercises of masters of an anguished sensuality like Louise Labé and Ausias March to the writer of pop songs. "You are too, too divine," Fats Waller used to sing with exaggerated passion to mock the nonsense lyrics that he was sometimes required to do, usually with a rolling of his eyes and nudging of the beat. The fact remains that sexual fantasies pursue us all, to good or bad effect, and bring us whole dramatic casts of men and women, either persons we know or would like to know or persons we hope never to meet in the flesh.

Sexual fantasies, peopling our imaginations with strangers and with familiars, can threaten us with their negativity as well as their positive assertions. Fantasies may possess us, may compel actions we regret but still stay enslaved to. Fetishes may embody barely perceptible fantasies in odd objects, a scarf, a belt, a shoe, a body part.[4] The same dominant fantasy plot may persist in us for decades, accompanying masturbation, not necessarily negative in itself, but giving rise to questions about its stubborn repetitiveness. Fearful fantasies about sexual diseases or infections may rouse our dread. Fantasies of loss and mourning may haunt our imaginings—of lovers who rejected us, of lovers who never received us in the first place, of a mate lost to death, divorce, illness. The sorrows around sexuality are sore ones and go deep. An unlived sexual life can do great harm, if it lies unclaimed and ungathered. A sexuality we ignore, treat carelessly and avoid, not one offered up in a generous celibacy but just left in unattended disrepair and disuse, falls all too heavily on those around us, especially upon children. Ordinary discourse between teacher and student, between parent and child, or between friends must carry the heavy burden of the undischarged excitement of unlived sexual life.[5] It usually shows as excessive irritability, a tendency to bickering, a withholding of response, or a chivying restlessness.

The people of our sexual imagination may be our unborn child or our newborn baby, one we look to in our fantasies to redeem or reform or recenter our whole life, the life that has so disappointed us. The child of such dreams is not left free to have its own problems but starts with the onus of having to carry its parents' problems, dimly hoping in a semiconscious way, to solve them in order to arrive at a beginning place in its own life.

In looking into our sexually imaginative population, we need to notice what sort of lens shapes our viewing. This means consciousness about our sexual stance and all the gender-making assumptions of our own time in our own culture. It is not enough to say, for example, that we have come out of the closet, free from the bonds of sexual prejudice. Are we looking through the lens of the lesbian, if that is what we claim as our posture, and if so, what particular personal shaping of a lesbian view? Is it one dominated by an image of the mother-daughter bond as the most defining and sacred of life, or the bond of the depths of female love? Or is it a stance shaped by the image of an all-female world, an Artemis image, where a man's view of a woman is experienced as a violating intrusion where "all wounds are male-created?"[6] Or is our lens a heterosexual one, and if so, which one?

Is it of a woman held within the father-daughter circle as protection against being reabsorbed by her mother? Is the woman struggling to find a sense of womanhood not defined by or equated to motherhood? Or is it the position of a man seeking connection to his father as one not only like himself, but bearing his full potential toward him, a relation of male depth to male depth, without any intervening rivalry over the mother-wife?

Whatever the lens through which we see and image human sexuality, it must reflect the influences of our own life in full detail, the assumptions about masculine and feminine of our culture, and the pressure of the particular archetypal images of sexuality that have come to bear upon our own body and psyche. Winnicott puts it in simple, clear fashion: "The principal factor which determines the way a child grows is the sex of the person the child is in love with at the critical age . . . after infancy and before the latency period." It is "extremely convenient," he says, if the child's sexuality develops along the lines of bodily endowment, "when a boy is mainly male, and a girl mainly female." He adds, "However, society gains much if it can tolerate the homosexual as well as the heterosexual in the emotional development of children."[7]

The Swiss psychoanalyst Alice Miller brings us to a similar conclusion from a different direction. To blame society's oppressive intolerance for our sexual difficulties detours us from consciousness. It is not the sicknesses that we can see through that make us ill, but the ones we cannot, the ones we took into ourselves at an early age, those imbalances bred by the confusions and intolerances of the parent we loved. So it is that a man who can only reach sexual gratification when looked on as contemptible is repeating with his wife what he began with his mother, if that was her attitude toward his instinctual life. The lens he is compelled to remake is what he must not merely notice but heed, for his compulsive action, so troublesome and time-consuming, is trying to bring to his attention the part of himself suffering under obsession and seeking to get free.[8]

To notice and pay attention to the lens through which we see our sexuality does not mean accepting what we find as irrevocable. Rather, what we are beginning to see is some of the complexity and allure of sexuality, what makes it so elusive and enhancing as well as troublesome. What we call our sexual stance or orientation reveals to us that sexuality itself, of whatever kind, is a lens, a way of seeing, a way of imagining. It is not a fixed commodity, but a means through which we live and transform our living, a lens for spirituality as much as for physiology. This is a fact brought home to us if our imagination knows its full share of lively turns and flexibilities. Sexuality is a principal way we view life as a whole, and death as a way we put ourselves into and take ourselves out of the worlds we share with others. Rather than a finality in a fixed position, we discover that our sexual identity is more a matter of improvisation—a gathering together of all the parts, the wounded places and fears as well as the capacities and pleasures, into a workable presence that we share in bodily terms as well as emotional and spiritual ones with our partners. The many bits and pieces that make up that presence come from the personal influences of women and men important to us, especially when we were young before our egos were formed from the dominant images of male and female in our culture, both bad and good, from all the images of masculine and feminine as ways of being human that have influenced us and continue to affect us.

This mosaic-like sexual identity protects us from falling into the gaps, between no identity and an ego-imposed one, between a prescribed identity enforced by family rule and an equally coercive one that comes from cultural tradition. We have become more and more familiar with the last danger in the late decades of the twentieth century. Women have been loud and clear about their objections to being fitted to prescribed roles, so often no more than male projections. Men have gradually come to take similar exception to being defined by cliché and stereotype. Gay and lesbian groups vociferously call attention to feeling marginalized by a heterosexual society. And any lover can testify from his or her experience just how limited any book on sexuality can be, especially if it is read as a recipe for positions, procedures, attitudes of mind, feelings of heart or gland, timings, tempos. There is no one prescribed method of sexual meeting in body or psyche or soul—only the great variety of human imaginings about all of them, tempered by the conscious experience of all.

Less clear are the dangers from the side of the gap where we try to impose a sexual orientation without acknowledging our dependence on our body, with all its characteristic qualities, and on the shaping influences of stages of our developmental growth. We are in things sexual as in other centers of our lives dependent in some measure on the persons we loved and hated, those who most influenced our growth, and upon the primordial images constellated in our unconscious, which inexorably bring their presence to bear on the ways we give sexuality its place in our imagination. As illustration, there is the student who believed in current cultural views that the human is androgynous more than it is male or female. He worked in a day-care center. One day a little boy asked him for help in going to the bathroom. He couldn't manage zippers. He asked his helper, Is this my penis and does that mean I am a boy and do you have one too? The student gave a definite unqualified Yes to all of the questions. He was struck, he said, by how important it was to sort out what you had in a body part and to which sex you belonged. No ambiguity would be helpful here, in the child's first contemplations. One episode with a little boy changed the student's ideas utterly.

The influence of archetypal images can be found in one woman's first pregnancy, in itself an accomplishment, for she had always been haunted by the fear she would not be able to have children. That dread arose from an only half-conscious subterranean interaction with her mother who on this level she felt to be life-killing. Her pregnancy and the approaching birth of a child accentuated her fantasies. A compensatory set of images from her unconscious surprised her. A long line of mothers, and mothers of mothers, presented themselves to her imagination, females linked back to the beginning of her family. Confiding herself to this long line of females who trusted in their instinct, she felt held, comforted, and strengthened for the coming birth. She knew rebirth in the birth.

This sort of identification of ourselves with others reaches across all sexual lines and provides us with rich imaginative resources. We are none of us complete in ourselves. In sexual development particularly we know incompleteness; with luck, we may end up knowing that dependence on the other brings the possibility of wholeness. At the phallic stage, for example, what Winnicott calls the phase of swank and strut for the male, a little girl feels less than a fully made or prepared female, partly because our culture makes no verbal acknowledgement of the vagina in the nursery room, partly because the potency of breast and womb have yet to assert themselves as they will at genital maturity.[9] When that last phase arrives, a male feels his incompleteness and genital dependence on the female.

The possibilities for the sexual roles of impregnation and giving birth, which identify male and female, have multiple imaginative counterparts. A man, for example, can cross-identify with a woman's maternal instincts and capacities. That will bring much to his life and to others, as he becomes a good male-mother who can tend children or nurture the growth of those who work with him or for him. More complicated, but even richer imaginatively, is a man's cross-identification with a woman's genital capacity as distinct from motherhood, not with her sexual role, now, but her actual body part. In Western culture women have been encouraged to know about and develop male modes of being. Less accepted and even more feared is the value accorded a woman who combines masculine and feminine ways of producing and reproducing. She stirs up a childish vision of the parent-monster, as Melanie Klein puts it, made up of both parents engaged in sexual intercourse. She is that monster, a being who contains both breast and penis potency, womb and cultural creativity.[10] Fear of this combined power underlies much of the discrimination against women, and the determination to keep them from equal pay and promotion possibilities. Why should women get both full-family and full-job lives? From such fear and resentment come attacks aimed at trying to make women choose between family and job, either by insisting on set hours at the office, or by refusing any rescheduling of work to meet pregnancy or child-rearing needs.[11]

No matter the difficulties, cross-identification has great appeal. It enriches the imagination by extending our capacities for sympathy and empathy, and makes it possible for us to put ourselves in the other persons' shoes, to go to deeper places. We imagine ourselves in other persons' bodies. This means we stand looking out at the world from a departure-point quite opposite to our conscious one of sexual identity. This is what Jung is getting at with his idea that we are contrasexual persons, not simply singularly male or female, with only univocal meanings where, for example, female equals maternity and male the one in charge, assumptions still operating in quantities of people of both sexes.[12]

To be contrasexual means to accept responsibility for a point of view based well within ourselves that may be very different from that of our conscious gender orientation. It means feeling inhabited by another point of view, one at odds to our accustomed perspective. If we repudiate it altogether, we invite fear. We feel invaded by a succubus or incubus that seems to tear away our life fluids. If we accept it imaginatively, and it is only imaginatively that we can possess the sexual organs opposite to those of our own, we move into remarkable experiences.[13] This sexual other that lives in us, we discover, not only gives us insight into a different departure-point; it roots us in the instinctive depths of everything human. A woman can expand to accept her own phallic thrusting, fighting, asserting dominance, pushing things through holes. A man can imagine his own secret pocket where he hides things inside himself, merging his blood with it, in tune with its privacy until it is ready to come forth.

This other starting-point of the sexual that lives in us is not the same in all of us, except for the fact that it is there. Its content varies greatly from person to person. Consciousness of this "other" within us pulls our consciousness toward the unconscious and reveals, of all things, how sexuality plays a central part in human spirituality.[14] The contrasexual other makes us conscious of the starting-point of life at the same time that it connects to its new and opposite departure-point. The double exposure decenters us, pulling the ego from center stage, and recentering us around a larger focus that takes ego views into consideration but subordinates them to the whole psyche. This is to arrive at what Jung calls the self, the personality larger than our egos.[15]

The people who fill our imagination, and especially those who carry the image of the other sex, figure centrally in our spiritual development. They pull our egos into the vast territory of the self. We imagine the otherness of the self through the foreignness of a body we do not have; we find a departure-point very different from our own. The "other" clothes itself in the symbolic form of a different anatomy. It introduces us to instinctive roots different from our accustomed ones, and pulls us toward the unconscious. The "other" becomes an image of depth.

We meet the other sides of our psyche, personified in images of a being opposite to our own sexual identity. A man weighed down with his responsibilities finds himself drawn right out of himself in fantasy by a woman to whom he is attracted in reality but cannot acknowledge except in cross-identifying imagination, one who is at once elusive and fiery, girlish and commanding in the passion she arouses in him. Another man finds his image of woman quite different. She is hard to find and harder still to get to. A highly arousing image comes to him, nothing like his unimaginative conscious musing about the opposite sex. When he imagines touching this woman sexually, he feels her on the ends of his fingers: "It's like opening a pistachio nut." A woman of introverted temperament repeatedly comes upon strong extroverted disdainful men in her dreams and finally sees these attitudes as her own: she herself does not give a rap for others' feelings and needs, but only wants to thrust her ideas into her world and have others submit to them. Another woman finds a different attitude hiding in herself, personified by a repeated dream sequence. Here a man of utter silence asserts nothing verbally, but only stands near her. She feels his breath upon her. The woman connects to this dream man's attitude and says it calms her, "earths" her.

What we all hope for is to be able, in Winnicott's words, "to risk nearly the full force of what is there in human nature."[16] That is what we count on artists for—to show us in music, paint, stone, words, dramatic action, or dance movement the full range of human experience. We accept every freedom in artists. They can move at will into both defined and undefined areas of human behavior, into an endless complexity of motivation and performance, of understanding and misunderstanding and enigma.

There is no rule that applies universally to everyone because "*imaginatively* there is surely no part of life that cannot be handed over or taken over."[17] Life is like art here; it can enrich itself in satisfying complexity almost without limit.

Consider for example, the imaginative richness that results from looking at something from this "other" point of view we find in ourselves. To do so at this point in history is usually to direct oneself to the feminine starting-point, because it has fallen so much into neglect and only now in the late years of the century is it being in some sense recovered. Take the example of a fairy tale, "Beauty and the Beast." What if the woman were the Beast and Beauty the male? In amorous play, he may then show softness and she the expected ferocity of a beast; he comes with sweet sounds, she with animal grunts. His skin may boast a silky touch and hers hairy roughness; he may open to receive and she look to fall upon him with teeth bared. Because, to follow the archetypal pattern of the tale, her father sold her for gain and security, and her siblings moved against her with envy, the woman must go a long way to find the lost ferocious aspect and work at its transformation in love.

On a larger scale, touching many more people, if we look at Freud's oedipal drama from the point of view of the women involved, a whole new light will be shed on the fabled Freudian reading of the ancient plot. In his mixing of myth and anthropology, the generation of the sons forms a primal horde under the domination of the father, who holds all under him in subjugation, most significantly the women of all generations. The sons both hate the father and love him, fear and revere him. They want to be like him and to displace him. Finally, the sons gang up on the father, kill him, eat him. They institute a prohibition against anyone assuming the father's place. They establish instead a fraternal organization. They set up this different image for the group, reflecting their fear that whoever succeeds the father will suffer the same fate, and also to show through this deferred obedience to the father their remorse for his murder. Shared social power and responsibility replace the model of a king with vassals subordinate to him. Women are no longer seen as the property of the ruler. The incest taboo enters: no woman of the same group can be taken as sexual partner by its males. They must seek sexual mates from other tribes.[18]

If we can imagine this scenario from the point of view of what has been left out, the female perspective, we see a remarkable transformation being enacted. Women who at first were just so much booty, prizes for the winner, now exist as sisters to brothers, as parts of the same social order, or as partners chosen from another group. They have come up in the world and offer us a new perspective. This way of looking helps us imagine the size of the sacrifice when male power and sexual dominance give way to shared social leadership. A masculine goal of ego-power and privilege shifts toward an imagination of kinship that plants the seeds of equality or, even more, a reversal of power. The image of woman as booty to be seized and possessed has been transformed into an image of a being chosen, sought after, brought home to personal relationship.

Which came first, the sacrifice of male power and privilege

or a different relation to the feminine that upset the configuration of subordinate to tyrant? When woman's place shifts, all, the whole lump is leavened. Even if we think of Freud's fantasy as applying only to the intrapsychic life of men, the pivotal place of the feminine holds. When she is seen, sought, and chosen, instead of simply negated and reduced to property, the man's vision enlarges from dominance to kinship, from a narrow singularity, lording it over others, to bonding with them. The feminine perspective yields startling social, political, and spiritual consequences.

Imagining reversals of our usual perspective through the departure-points of our cross-identification, with persons and attitudes far different from our own, brings us to a major question: How does living with the people in our imaginations contribute to our hope for passion in enduring relationships with real people? Hope for recovery from destructiveness, whether in ourselves or others, and the guilt that goes with it have a lot to do with our sexuality and our spirituality. And both have a strong place in our imagination. How can we live with an "other" in a way that includes both excitement and reliability? This question, which puzzles our minds and ignites our fantasies, is the great question for marriage or any other kind of long-term relationship that must involve bodily excitement and sharing to survive. Friendships also move into this terrain, but less boldly, because the sexuality in them is not lived out in the same way.

We come together in relationships for all sorts of reasons, and not always the best. We may marry to escape loneliness, to find the father who will never abandon us, or to prove we can be a father, to plant all that nurturing zeal we feel in someone, to construct a functional family to offset our original dysfunctional family, to finally possess something of our own, which we can act out with our children and through them, to find a place to break down or to break out, to hold onto someone who looks likely to put us in touch with a lost part of ourselves. Or, simply enough, we can marry to have children, for companionship, for passion.

Whatever the reasons for wanting and entering a long-term

partnership, the question remains, Does this relationship bring excitement along with reliability? Can we live creatively in this relationship and also make the necessary adjustments and compromises that two different psyches must present, especially after there are children? The coming of a baby poses an enormous threat to its parents. Their absorption in this new life, coupled with their exhaustion in taking care of it, threatens to turn the man and woman away from all they have shared together, to reduce them to banalities, to Mom and Pop routines. Gone is the spiritual and sexual excitement between them, submerged under their fascination with and labor for the child that now draws to itself all their projections of hope, of new being and new beginnings. But then there is the fortunate child who grows up in a household where the parents' love for each other has lost none of its sexual passion. The whole household is infused with a quiet excitement that gives a child its own hope and pleasurable expectation for a life of its own.

To allow for excitement in an ongoing committed relationship means to act and respond out of impulse, need, desire, idea, not simply in compliance with others' expectations or the responsibilities for others we project onto others, especially our mates. Excitement includes instinct, tension, and the imaginative elaboration of bodily experiences so that we come to expect something, and look for it, and if necessary create it. Like Winnicott's description of a child's moments of illusion, where she has created something she has found and thus gained the capacity to believe in reality and risk, crossing the border between what is actually in the world and what she imagines exists in it, we too can have our rich productive illusory moments. We can do things, think things, feel things, imagine things that feel intensely real and original to us, have moments where we feel we have created what happened or at least made our contribution to it. This is excitement. This is living creatively. We can reject, then, with absolute ease the dispiriting advice, "Now it is time to settle down into your mature years." We can understand a woman's spontaneous answer to the question of how long she has been married, "Not long enough!" even though it has been twenty years. We can laugh with the man who insists on calling his wife on his car phone from the driveway to his house as he comes from work, despite the inconvenience this causes, which he can see clearly enough through the kitchen window as he watches her rushing to the phone, dropping their child's dishes, looking nervously at pots boiling on the stove. Nonetheless, he insists on calling her to the phone, and imagine, just to tell her to come outside and look at the full moon!

Even if our life lacks this element of excitement we hold its images in our minds until we can reach it with our partner. Somehow we must risk reaching through our own deadened state. A wife bemoans her husband's lack of forcefulness. He even suffers impotency at times. Then she discovers in her forays through her imagination, her fear of her own aggressiveness, so large that it acts to lock up his aggression as she puts pressure on him, in effect, to supply a double dose of the precious force. She complains that their life together lacks zest. It succeeds wonderfully, one would say, in a functional way, balancing two careers, two children. Their marriage is in fact a job well done, but it reflects no passion, no sheer gladness in their being together. On the rare occasions her husband opens his own fears to her, his worries and secret ambitions, to her horror she finds herself going blank. Panic grips her. Why this? She fears two things, that his fears are her fault, his problem really hers, and that she will have to fix everything. She would rather not know what is broken. To protect herself she blanks out, effacing the moment of delicate trust between them, making it lifeless. She feared her own impulses to comfort him lest she lose herself, and her own impulses to challenge him to reach toward his best self, lest she destroy him. The people of her imagination represent her unowned, untamed, great compassion and her vigorous appetite for an aggressive wrestling with life. She has not known how to give it to her husband because she has not fully taken it for herself.

To most people excitement in relationships means something sexual but is not confined to that realm. What is unlived may find residence in our imaginations to be brought out later under safer conditions and in a quite different form, as those of great sensuality, for example, find themselves moved toward the spiritual life. What is urgent is to accept the existence of a fantasy life, to acknowledge that much of it has a sexual character, and that the sexual imagination has large transforming powers. It may deepen and enlarge a relationship. It may open a new one. If we do not recognize it, if, as so many do, we disavow it, we all too easily move to act it out without even knowing that we are doing so. It is in that zone of near unconsciousness that morality is shed and judgments become untrustworthy.

The sexual imagination, as we have tried to show in these pages, is at the very least a force for honesty in our lives. Its large presence, acknowledged, even greeted, has great strengths. Faced directly, brought to consciousness, it offers a sharpening of identity, the possibility of relationship, the reality of every kind of love. The force of the experience is nowhere better communicated than in that extraordinary moment, as Luke's gospel describes it, after the annunciation, when Mary visits Elizabeth. Elizabeth, a woman of some age, is now in the sixth month of pregnancy after years of barrenness. Elizabeth meets Mary first with the salutation that we know as part of the Hail Mary prayer and then with her splendid acknowledgment of her own glowing sexuality: "For behold, when the voice of your greeting came to my ears, the babe in my womb leaped for joy." We should remember that meeting and those words as an icon of the sexual imagination and all that it represents.

Desire, according to Hegel, is a generalized form of consciousness. It testifies to the existence of our senses. It makes us, for positive or negative purposes, conscious of the existence of a self. Even "the unhappy consciousness," in some of the least satisfactory experiences of desire, finds in itself "the inner certainty of its self, and that its feeling of real being is this self-feeling." What then is the feeling that accompanies an Elizabeth after the double annunciation—Mary's, that pivotal moment for Christianity and all religion, and her own, when the baby John the Baptist leaps in her womb? Being is confirmed. Animal and spiritual desire are conjoined. Consciousness presupposes desire. Desire is the sign of the self and all the conscious and unconscious worlds that the self can lead to. In desire begins faith.

That is what the sexual imagination tells us, if we heed it in its most telling moments. The great Spanish poet Juan Ramón Jiménez in the sequence of 57 poems called *God Desired and Desiring* tells the tale in verses of an astonishing limpidity. He desires his "god still to come," his god of "beauty accomplished," the god of his own "consciousness of the beautiful." But his god is already with him, in his "electric zone/as in love all love is to be found." God is present as the special example and mirror of his imagination and of his "imagination in movement." God was, God is, God came, in the acts of becoming, in the ancient elements, earth, air, fire, water. God is love in the poet's "body of a man and in the body of a woman." The involutions are indescribable and yet somehow describable. The poet says to his god, "I am the wrapping round my center/of you inside it." He describes God's voice as "white fire," recalling Ignatius of Loyola's way of characterizing his experience of the primordial presence as whiteness, whiteness, always whiteness.

Everything is "directed at this *tesoro palpitante*," this burning pulsating treasure. The language leaps with feeling, sexual and spiritual, as Jiménez finds consciousness of heights—of tide, of sky, of God, of ecstasy. In a mixture of Dante and John of the Cross, in the ten terse lines of "*Que se ve ser*" (Seeing its Being), he confronts "A being of light, who is all and only light." In his inversion of the dark night of the soul, his god turns into a diamond-like consciousness and a burning-hot white coal, *en la mañana oscura*, in the dark morning.

Here, in these meditations, in this pilgrimage of his imagination, he has found the most direct access of his "fated" desire. He knows God as God and God as himself, as the poet, and has felt such a joy in being as to make him shout "that I was I." He sees God not only leading him but desiring him. The cross-identification of his sexual imagination leads him to his own annunciation:

I am your entrails
and within them I move
as in the air, and never am I smothered;
I will never be smothered in your nest
as a child does not drown in the womb
of his mother. . . .

He cannot be smothered, cannot drown in God's entrails, God's womb, for they are his, too, as God is in his blood and in his breathing. He is altogether "penetrated," transfixed, by the loving tenderness of what he has seized with his presence.

With our consciousness, Jiménez says, we can love anything, monsters included, for our consciousness moves easily among those with whom we share our likeness and our image. Walking with God, we walk with ourselves. In our fantasies, we rest in the heat of our love for a "desiring god" in "this nest in our deep interior." Everything is brought together, as he says so simply, so brightly, in a prose poem, "The Naked Infinite," as with man joined to woman, which is what the name of woman signifies, *los dos en uno, en una,* "the two in the one man, in the one woman." God is not a terminus but an open intention, an aim, a being, as the poet is, too, a "beautiful consciousness in the oneness that is made of two." God is Jiménez's tabula rasa, a white page mirroring an open mind, one who "throbs with the color of my time."

The three central points of his life, the standards by which to judge it, Jiménez says in his notes for *God Desired and Desiring,* are woman, work, and death. They turn around in his consciousness as he tries to understand how high in the realm of the divine "the human can reach by the grace of being human," and how much of the divine can be taken in through human effort, how we can achieve our highest ends by our gathering of what we have bestowed on the god made flesh. Beauty, consciousness, his nest deep inside him, the womb of his presence—these are the terms of the poet's imagination, these are the fruits of his desire. It is the *Camino de Fé,* as he calls it in the preface to the book, the path, the way, of faith. It is what will bring him to join the good thief in the Paradise Jesus promised the thief. Death itself is acceptable in such an exercise of the consciousness that desire brings, in such a movement of the imagination. "I am going," says the poet, "to his word beyond the Book," that is, transcending even scriptural words, "as to a field of daisies in the human spring, or as to a mirror of light in the human winter."[19]

Chapter 6

Who Feeds the Feeder?

Why should we even ask the question? Because joining the so-called helping professions carries such dangers. To offer help is to enter deep waters. Preaching, teaching, and counseling, social work, chaplaincy, psychotherapy and all the others are depleting to all who work at them. One can all but perish from burnout or burn-up. Rescue and healing demand the imagination. It brings food to the exhausted soul.

For burning out amounts to exhaustion. We have not one thing more to give, or even to think or feel or hope. We are gutted, by the problems, needs, demands, suffering, and resentment brought to us in such eagerness. Unlike jobs that can be left behind in the office at quitting time, here we know no limits of time or energy or pre-occupation. The ministry in particular, standing-in as it does for God's love and care, rouses people's expectations that the pastor will appear at any time, if a crisis occurs, even in the middle of the night, even if it interrupts a long-awaited vacation. Who else can do my wife's funeral? People do not die on schedule, or break down, or reach out only between the hours of nine and five, with time off for lunch.

In the face of such unending need, there can only be unending drain. Didn't Jesus say, The poor you will always have with you? Doesn't that mean the poor in spirit as well as in body, the poor in mental health as well as in social advantage? The biggest drain on any professional helper is the omnipresence of failure. Even if we succeed we fail, for whatever gets done amounts to so little. Discouragement regularly lays siege to our will. Despair and cynicism take root. Over a lifetime, we are worn down, worn out. We discover that we have nothing left to give. We feel empty, a husk without fruit. In consciousness, we feel eaten alive; at an unconscious level, as if robbed, utterly drained by the needs of others. This often proves a source of marital strife or of conflict with friends. The helper uses himself up in the service of others at the sacrifice of his intimate relationships—with child, lover, mate, friends. Nothing is left over for personal relationships. The emotional cupboard is bare.

What happens in our personal life comes to seem pallid, trivial, compared with the larger-than-life crisis situation, the intensity of engagement in these moments of life and death. How can an ordinary quarrel, even the richest, toughest, most demanding exchange, compete with the pure malice of a hate-filled transference in a counseling relationship? How can helping a child puzzle through alternative choices at school command the same intensity of attention as a parishioner threatening suicide?[1] Yes, we can get hooked on the highs of ministry and all its surrogates. The preacher lapses into orotund public voice over the dinner table. The teacher lays out all the fine steps to the concluding classroom argument for her family. The spiritual director suddenly goes pious when religious matters are discussed, eyes oozing unction, just waiting to be asked for his wisdom. Behind all these addictions to powerful poses lie despair and impotence in the face of so much misery and need. We burn out because we give our best again and again, and again and again fail to cure the illness. It is like trying to end once and for all the illness of bad housing or corrupt city planning. Illness in unfed psyche and soul, illness in ignorance and unnurtured faith has no quick fix.

From a chronic sense of failure to make any lasting difference, professional helpers can become angry at all the projections heaped upon them. People expect soothing from their substitute parents more than they would from their real ones, endless handouts, bottomless forgiveness. People expect their clergy to take all the heat and show of temper they can bring without retaliating. Just make things better for us. Fix this imperfect world. And damn it, be sure you're always interesting in the pulpit, wise in the counseling room. Show us the way. Nothing else works? Then take our place and suffer for us. He did, didn't He? With such a barrage of conscious and unconscious expectations, no wonder clergy are so often enraged at their congregations.

The case is self-evident, it seems to us, for training clergy in the ways of the unconscious. We must make sure they know about projection and introjection, and how some people defend themselves by splitting off the bad and putting it onto someone else, such as that convenience, their minister. If we are training clergy to go into the trenches, then we need to give them ammunition—and the best ammunition is consciousness. They must be made aware of their own problems as well as of the psychic mechanisms by which we defend ourselves, themselves included. For one of the shortest ways to burn out and then turn angry or cynical, is to identify ourselves as the helpers with all the good stuff to give and the recipients of our help as possessing all the bad.[2] We fall into a kind of omnipotence of benevolence. We excise from consciousness all our own negative feelings and power drives. The dedicated helper takes on the role of omnipotent feeder, with an endless supply of milk or advice or love, leaving the helped with all the hate and despair. Worse still, we defend against the bad in ourselves by playing the role to the hilt. We will manage, we will cure all the ailing others, not seeing that we have in fact left them paralyzed in an infantile and hopeless position, never recognized, with nothing of their own to contribute. The only way they can assert their right to being a person is to thwart our helping, because getting helped means playing a role, too, always sickeningly grateful to and dependent upon the benevolent helper.

In such situations, goodness itself departs, moved out of reach of both helper and helped. We all exist together as sinners. None of us possesses the good. Goodness, we must remember, exists only as something to be shared among us. It is not an abstraction. It is not a thing, something one holds in measurable qualities and parcels out to others.

Burnout results from causes which recall our image of the gap. We may make an idol of our way of preaching, teaching, counseling, or spiritual direction. We become identified with it, and like Cinderella's sisters try to force others to accept our magic standpoint. With our method of preaching we will succeed and our congregation will find the true path. With this developmental theory, we can chart exactly where our clients are stuck psychologically and where they can find release. With our method of prayer, we can induct others into the mysteries of the Holy Spirit. With this course of teaching, we can make the truth lucid to our students. And on and on we go. Rhetoric masks inflation and bullying. All lively connection disappears.

Our congregation either merely complies, which may look like polite listening but in fact covers a tuning-out of real response, or it just leaves the church or temple, if not the whole religious enterprise. A congregation knows very soon—almost by a primitive sense of smell—whether its priest, minister or rabbi is reaching to the depths or even struggling to reach them. A congregation's psyches and souls will defend it almost automatically against anything less. Teachers and pastors do not have to know all the answers, but they have to want to know. They have their own struggling to do, with their own god-images and their own relationship to God. When we make an idol out of our god-image and bully others to accept it, we offer a stone instead of bread.

Bullying can come from trying to foist a private god-image into the public arena as God, or from insisting that only the official god-images decreed by tradition are valid. We have seen both of these swings in the last decades of our century. Causes for women, for races, for ecology, for psychology, ideologies of all kinds have been thrust into worship as images of God. God is red, dead, black, female, gay, revolutionary, psychic or sociological force. In contrast, we have seen specific old images of God legislated as the only true ones, with little or no effort to connect them to the people who are asked to believe in them. A few static images of the Trinity, images of the Father, a Christology insisted upon as the only true religion vie with ways of performing the sacraments. Only a very modern vernacular is acceptable. Or, for a small number, the truth is locked in Latin. A believer is left with no guiding shepherd, no wonderful counselor, no friend in the Spirit.

One of the unexpected ways we burn out is through what

we would call burn-up. We burn right through god-images that consume us with their intensity. These images are lively parts of our tradition, or constructions of our own psyches and souls. It may be, as it was for a while, the introduction of guitars into the mass. It may be concelebration or a determined introduction of social issues into every sermon, every parish bulletin, every church meeting. Our energies are dedicated to our images of God and the Holy as redeemers of a world lost in injustice and imbalance. We use up our strengths in serving what might well be good concerns. We feel spit out, spent, left empty.

Burn-up can also come from success. Most clergy develop their own good ways of working. Their very effectiveness brings them to the limits of the approach or method they use. They tire of it; they cannot perform any more. They reach the end of what is in effect a working image of the divine in our midst. They burn it up. Similarly in prayer, or teaching, or preaching, or a style of administration, our very success brings us an abrupt summons to change. We must exercise our imagination as if our lives depended upon it, for they do. We must grow or die, find the new or collapse, burnt up, burnt out.

The fact that we can burn up from success is a puzzling aspect of consciousness. As the circle of our awareness widens, the perimeters of our unconsciousness also increase. The larger the scope of knowing, the larger the circumference of unknowing. The more we hone our skills the closer we come to the borders of the wilderness where there are no markers, no skills. Either we go on, into that place beyond the boundaries, or we burn out. But going into the unknown poses a great risk, the risk of consciousness of self. Jung said that we would do almost anything rather than know ourselves.[3]

Burnout and burn-up join. The unlived life that we refuse to live, like the helper who claims to be all good, with nothing bad, just a bundle of help, ignores the hidden power-motive in so much of our helping. That life waiting to be lived seeps into our relations with those we are out to help and poisons them, hurting all of us, reducing the help to nothing. But there is also that unlived life that simply stays untouched, unnoticed, unapproached. This is not the world of repression, where hidden power-drives lurk. This is unentered, unsought, unknown territory. When its unlived life is evoked, which will happen inexorably when we have lived through what we really know of life, then we must respond quickly, directly, with full acknowledgment or feel the full force of burn-up, consumed by what is offered to us. Let us take a strong example.

A woman pastor of a small church exercised a style of ministry so successful it doubled her congregation. Her style felt feminine to her. She was facilitating the work of others in the church, engendering their enthusiasm and initiative. Tasks were shared. But the very success of her style pushed her to a new place of heightened consciousness, where now she knew what it was to feel poor in spirit and pitched into the gap of fear, doubt, and agonizing distress. The successful building campaign, the opening of the church house to an Alzheimer program four days a week, the request for additional prayer- and Bible-study groups, all combined to press her to develop a new mode of leadership in herself where suddenly she felt weak and doubting and insecure. She needed to speak out more, to stand out more, to exert her authority through a willingness to give her own opinions and take the heat of others' reactions to them. She felt she had to use some masculine side of herself, not in place of her feminine style, but in addition to it. If she refused she knew she would burn up, would exhaust her old style of ministry. The tasks that required her individual leadership included things specifically directed to her own benefit, like proposing the parsonage be sold to accrue funds for all the pastors to come, to buy their own home, but beginning with herself. She needed to argue the case for an associate pastor to help her with the increased workload. This assertive style was not freely available to her. She could not find in herself the ability to see a goal and go straight for it. She needed to uncover aggression, buried under repression. Her aggression frightened her as it began to emerge from the shadows and it took some time for her to find her own way of combining it with her old, softer, more conventionally feminine, engendering style of ministry. She did finally come to a combination of styles she summed up in a phrase: to assert the good we have in common.

Burn-up may be the cost of our attempts to come close to the divine presence. What an odd problem—just from coming too near the source of being! It is a living all over again of some of the terrors of the Old Testament. We forget the anchor of our own psyches and souls and move right toward the fire. For preachers to be open all at once to their own god-images and to those of their congregation, to the images of God in scripture and tradition, and to try imaginatively to link them all up, is to come dangerously near the primordial fire. It can incinerate. The clergy know a double vulnerability, to familiar human experiences of the divine and to the God never really captured in either personal or traditional images. In a sense the clergy, whose job it is to be preoccupied with images of God, hangs from the cross of warring forces. It is to live like one of the thieves, stretched on their crosses, pulled in opposite directions, but still eager, like Prometheus, to steal the fire from the gods and give it to their people.[4] Which thief are we, then; the one who mocked or the one who wanted to be with Jesus in heaven? It is a crucial work of the imagination to determine the answer. Our spiritual life, which is to say our whole life, depends upon it.

Our days secure their distinction in the thoughts and feelings, the people and places and things, to which our imagination takes us. We add or subtract color through our imagination. We find drama this way, suspense, depth. It can be the drama of the soap opera or the passion. We can live vicariously the reductions and falsifications of *Dallas* or *Dynasty*, or the reality of the gospels. You will say, if a preacher confronts you with this choice, that it is itself a reduction and a falsification. No one, surely, takes that nonsense seriously; that's just a silly little entertainment, to bring a moment of inconsequential pleasure to our days —or nights. The preacher who has associated himself or herself with the good thief—or Prometheus—must disagree. Our imagination is always with us. If we fill it with silly little entertainments, which millions, let it be said, take very seriously, we move it far from its moorings in being. We develop dreams and fantasies of cutthroat competition, for oil, for multinational conglomerates, for men, for women. Fed by such empty tales and the shell-like people who inhabit them, our appetite demands more and more violence, of which there is an unending supply in film and book as well as television. We look for escape from the nagging routines and petty sufferings of our lives and find it in the unvarying hedonism and gargantuan pandering to self of the polyester pop arts.

The imagination deserves better. It is, like it or not, want it or not, our way to being. If our experience of the secondary imagination, to use Coleridge's terms again, is at the level of soap opera, our understanding of the primary, of the infinite I Am, will be something in the range of a glistening robot, an actor or actress suspended between toupee and cosmetic. Otherness will become the work of the make-up man. Our capacity for sympathy and love will be wasted on polyester creatures blustering and festering under the assaults of nylon problems, and soon we will be without much of the resource for the real thing.

The world of experience to which the good thief and the preacher call us is not at all synthetic. Christ on the cross is the image of the work of one's days and the suffering of one's life put to the utmost good use. It is an opening to meaning where there might otherwise be meaninglessness. It is purpose personified. Nothing, we are told with this drama, is aimless, without substance, without value. It does not take a great imagination to see this; it simply requires the willingness to use some imagination. The subject is complex. It covers all the possible purposes to which a life may be put. But for all its complexity, it comes down finally to one comparatively simple point, the point of life which we face when we face death. Has it made any sense to have been alive, to have been? Here, now, at the end of life, do we face nothing, do we see nothing, do we say nothing? Is it all an absurdity? Have we come at the last to the edge of a precipice from which we drop into everlasting nothingness, into an eternal zero? Has all this endurance, the learning, the loving, the dieting, the dentists, the doctors, the prayers, the misery, the job, been a senseless delusion? Christ on the cross says no. Even more emphatically, because with so much less understanding, so does the good thief.

One does not even have to be a Christian to accept this. One simply has to have an imagination, and the courage, like the good thief, of one's imagination. We are all like the thief on Jesus's right, or Boethius in his cell or Sir Thomas More in his, condemned to die. Unlike those worthies, most of us do not know exactly when our death will come. We are not, most of us, capable of producing a dialogue with an incarnation of wisdom, like Boethius's *Consolation of Philosophy,* or that other self-inquiry at the point of death of a falsely accused man, More's *Dialogue of Comfort Against Tribulation.* But in our dungeons and towers, all of us can look into ourselves with whatever gifts or skills are at our disposal. All of us have enough imagination to join these men, however little we may think of ourselves, however far from being saints we may believe ourselves, in practicing the presence of death. We must, to see sense and structure in our lives, to refuse the reduction of all that we have done and all that we have been to an absurdity, look for the moments, at the very least in our imagination, where our lives are threatened and we must, like the good thief, answer for them.

Something in us already inclines toward the practice of the presence of death, whether we realize it or not, are willing to put it in such terms or not. What, after all, are we doing when we bring ourselves, with full participation, to sit through those interminable cheerfully terrifying chase sequences at the end of the Indiana Jones movies or thrust ourselves yet again into the bloody encounters in outer space of the *Star Wars* films or the endless Armageddon of the androids, *Star Trek?* What keeps us coming to the utterly implausible shootouts in the buddy-cop or rival-cop movies, each one pushing violence to nastier, more deranged, more fruitless extremes? That violence, depicted in such meticulous and loving detail, defies the science not only of human reflex behavior but of weapon design. The situations are often ridiculous or unbelievable, the characterizations inane, the underlying assumptions about human motivation intolerable, a far worse reading of the psyche and soul of the villain and his pursuers than anything ever dreamt of in the classical encounters of Westerns. And yet audiences keep coming back for more, insist, if only vicariously, on facing the worst of violent deaths. It is the drama of the cross reduced to the size of an emaciated imagination. But it remains that great drama, however thinned out and enfeebled. We ask ourselves this way, at some remove from full consciousness, basic questions about the value of life. We insist on placing ourselves, in however contrived and unfulfilling a fashion, in those perils which make us contemplate life and death, and we ask our ministers to do the same, for themselves and for us.

The work of ministry requires one to put oneself in such places where one's entire safety is in jeopardy. We can lose our god-images, as they are simply consumed by the holy presence. We can lose our hold on the images given us in scripture. They too can be consumed in the burning encounter. What are we left with then? A great darkness. An unknowing silence, vastness, muteness, where we can no longer speak for the Holy as we have been hired to do. And yet even in this dark unknowing silence, it speaks, and speaks through us.

Can we risk such a spectacle? What if nothing comes, what if nothing does speak through us? What then? What if we refused to be like either of the thieves on the cross? What if we tried to cash in like Judas on our knowledge of things spiritual, not with pieces of silver but in the coin of great preaching or supreme help of our ineffable spiritual authority? Who then pays the price? Perhaps the church, perhaps members of our family, those nearest us, those dependent on us. Under the pressures of a priest's zealousness, his or her family falls apart. The preacher succeeds and the child fails. The preacher is known for profound religious understanding and his or her child is delinquent. The rabbi is known for great learning and his or her child drops out of school. The minister is known for spiritual wisdom and his or her child commits suicide.

These are not light or passing things, but burning wounds. It is risky to come before God, but it is the first order of business and we have no business coming before others as clergy without first coming before God. We can be sure that if we take the profession of faith seriously that the dangers of pulling away and drying up, or of pulling near and getting lost in the currents of unfathomable mystery, must beset us. The stresses and strains of the spiritual life will touch weak places in ourselves and we may feel madness very near to us. The goal of the religious life, for any of us, is to draw as near as all that and to somehow survive it.

What and who feed the feeder depend on the feeder's own conception of what is food. No matter how different we are from one another, we share the same needs to be fed. But by what, by whom? It is imagination's task to discover what nourishes us in all our particularity. Beginning with the simplest acknowledgment of what we like to eat, in literal fact and in our imagination, is to take the first step away from the burning. This means a constant interview with the self, turning over in fantasy what really feeds us, which is to say what really matters to us, what so far as we can formulate it we live for. This amounts to trying to put into words and pictures, no matter how awkward, something about the nature of the human psyche and soul, and not abstractly, but in our own living of our own life. We need to ask finally what we are doing our jobs for, why it matters to us to try to understand or try to do something about another's puzzlement or emptiness or physical suffering. These questions push us periodically into groupings, causes, conferences, seminars with each other, to learn and share what we find. We are not defining formulas but imaginatively stretching as far as we are able, in human range, in physical strength, in spiritual reach toward that mysterious sense of personhood.

Religious training reminds us that health alone is not our goal. Being alive, feeling real, living imaginatively make the difference between a life that feels wasted and one that seems worth living. Psychological development, political freedom, environmental provisions sustain a full life, but religion tells us they are not enough to engage us at the center of our lives. We are instructed bluntly: the good life, the real life, is lived in relation to God. Thus the constant interviewing of ourselves can lead again away from the burning out or up. Our questions coalesce now around the central one: How can we live close to meaning? In religious language, how can we notice and correspond with grace, today's, yesterday's, on our way home in the car, on the subway, walking across the field, driving on the freeway? How can we take in and live with grace?

This sort of question, rooted in the imagination, directs us to our unfinished business—all those problems that lay siege to our sanity and our confidence. These are the problems that have persisted for years. This is where we face the stubborn splits in our character, the repeating fantasies, the dream motifs that recur, the fears and anxieties that we have been afraid to acknowledge, to understand, even to name, which continue to plague us. These problems may arise with new things arriving at consciousness, with a primitive compulsiveness that will not retire, with all the infectious energy that accompanies a passage from the unconscious to consciousness. These places of unlived life are doors which cannot be locked, through which the otherness of life reaches. These are the forces of our psychic growth, which spawn problems that make it necessary for us to change, to expand, to relocate ourselves on our journey. These are the tasks that the gods lay upon us, and these places may just be where God has contrived to meet us. Jung puts it this way: "The serious problems in life are never fully solved. If they ever should appear to be it is a sign something has been lost. The meaning and purpose of a problem seems to lie not in its solution but in our working at it incessantly. This alone preserves us from stultification and petrification."[5]

Each of us needs to find our particular way to work—and incessantly, as Jung says—with these problems and to bring our unlived life into open play. The routes are many. If we refuse to find which one belongs to us we end up eating our students, our clients, our congregations, instead of feeding them and feeding with them on the great source of being that has been made available to us.

To find our route we need imagination, because it is not imitation that is asked for but improvisation. What is demanded is our own combination, bringing together what presses in on us from the unconscious and what we find at hand in our personal inheritance, in our tradition. Counselors need to bring to awareness their own religious belief systems, whatever underlies their methods of treatment. Only then, by wrestling with their own myths of meaning, can counselors hope to hear from clients what are the myths *they* live by. Religious experiences and convictions are often the last thing to be confided to a therapist.

Sexual life in copious detail, money problems, a fear of violent feeling—all of this comes quickly enough. The quiet feelings in a quiet voice, after the whirlwinds of sex and aggression, are confided only when a deep trust in a shared experience develops. For that to happen, a counselor must be occupied with his or her own struggle to span imaginatively the gap between a dream, say, where he or she worshipped a pig and a conscious, less bizarre worship of the God of the fourth gospel.[6] We display what we believe through the way we choose to integrate what comes to us from our gaps.

Sometimes meeting this imaginative task leads a professional back into therapy. Sometimes it is possible, as a result of the struggle, to mark an end to work already done. In that case, if we continue to listen to and record our dreams and fantasies, we find a new otherness introduced into our daily discourse with ourselves. For the language of the unconscious always tells us what is actually happening to us, not what should be or what we would like to have happen.[7] Dreams as the principal language-in-ordinary of the unconscious always ground us in the muddy earth from which we have grown—the mud of infantile fears, of our conflicts and grandiose ambitions. They bring us intimations from the most far-flung distances of a wholeness that summons us into being. We dream of the most prosaic things, of laundry and bowel movements, for example, and we dream of sounds so celestial that they bid us leave off all the usual inner racket of anxious thoughts, nagging worries, boring tasks, to follow this grand thrumming into a new sense of the universe. One man dreamt such a sound in the image of a monastery in the woods where the round of worship sounded like so many bees buzzing their praise of the Lord. The beckoning may be visual or even olfactory. One woman dreamt she was in a huge house in the middle of a city, in a large square marble foyer. At its entrance stretched gigantic beds of peonies, hundreds of them, pink, rose and white, fully open. She said she could almost smell their fragrance. It was a moment of absolute beauty. Time came to a stop. All that had ever been existed here, in this blossoming moment.[8]

Otherness comes through other people, too. If we are lucky

enough to have friends who are good enough to tell us when we are talking nonsense and to make clear that they love us anyway, we will know ourselves richly fed. Even mourning for a lost friendship can feed us, as we search for what went wrong. One man finally found an explanation in a dream of a lost friendship. The paradox of the dream plot matched the ambivalences and ambiguities of his old friends' denials that the friendship was lost, denials that had so confounded him. Inexplicably, his friends, a married couple, had seemed unable or unwilling to make the effort to see him. The dream at last brought him a sense of resolution and closure. He dreamt he had given his friends something of great value. They were glad to have it, welcomed it. Much later in the year, in the winter, it was clear he was to go to their house in the dead of night and take back his gift. It was as if he were a thief, but he clearly was not a thief. They wanted him to take it back but did not want to acknowledge their desire to have him do so. He went. It was dark. The lawn before their house was covered with snow, a cold cover for a dying relationship. He took back his gift. They knew he was doing so, but wanted not to know. It was better for them, and for him, to pretend it had been stolen.

Still a different road away from burnout and burn-up is to put ourselves into situations which are completely different from our accustomed ones. Martin Buber once recommended to an analyst famous for her work with schizophrenics, herself suffering keenly from burnout, that she go to another part of the country where she was not known. "Take a room or rent a house," he said, "and live there for six weeks, no longer as Dr. So and So, but merely as the woman you are. Just live there."[9] A similar prescription is to take up a language from a distant culture, even one with a different alphabet, such as Russian, Greek, or Japanese. Or listen to nothing but the Bartok quartets or Schoenberg. A student offers the best example. She was a middle-aged woman of professional accomplishment and spiritual discernment. Feeling the need for the replenishment of her aching soul, she put herself in a class to learn tap dancing. She even joined in the year's recital with all the youngsters who made up the class. The best students were placed in the first row. And then there she was, towering in the back row, looming over her little classmates, neat and shining in their tutus.

Otherness often comes to us through our bodies; thus the absolutely right course for that woman—tap-dancing. Some people find their replenishment in systematic physical exercise, excellent as long as it does not become just another accomplishment to be acquired—so many miles to jog, so many seconds to raise one's heart beat, so much fiber to stimulate one's bowels.

Not for clergy alone, but for almost all of us, the food must be sought in some kind of spiritual reading. To risk entry into the wilderness, which any concerted prayer-life will lead to sooner or later, one needs as friends those who have gone before us. There is a wide range of possibility. We should be led by our interest wherever it goes, but never miss our daily feeding. Exposure to the vastness of the other side waiting for us needs recognizable voices, familiar ones, comforting ones, so that we do not lose our nerve, or worse, fall into despondency or despair.

When we pray, we talk to God, St. Augustine says, but when we do spiritual reading, God talks to us. He was speaking of the consecrated texts of the fathers who had preceded him and of scripture. In the millennium and a half since Augustine, the numbers of such texts, starting with his own incomparable contribution, have mounted to the size of a great library. It is only too easy to feel overwhelmed, not to know where to begin. But the great texts are unmistakable, it seems to us, filled with the understanding, the comfort, the boldness, and the mixture of the practical and the exalted which assures us of the presence of the ultimate.[10]

Not every one will speak to us directly. One text may be caught in the rhythms of a time so far removed from ours that we just cannot feel its pulse. Another may seem artificial in its rhetoric or sentimental or impossibly demanding. If the text is meant for us, we will know it quickly. Distant in time or just around the corner, it will tell us something about ourselves, it will make the struggle for self-understanding easier to bear, it will bring us the consolation of joining with a great soul in the struggle. We will find ourselves associating with an Augustine, a

Pascal, a Jacob Boehme, a Catherine of Genoa, a Berdyaev, a Thérèse of Lisieux, and for something like pages at a time on equal terms.

We will not be suffering from delusions of grandeur. We will simply be joining the spiritual combat right in the midst of the fray. It is a brawl and always has been. The large figures of the life of the spirit know this and never let us forget it, not to make us feel bad, not to scold, and never, never to allow themselves or those for whom they write either to fall into discouragement or to take simple unrealistic comfort. They are tough-minded, realistic, loving, practical. "Nowadays, everyone is constantly questioning the good faith of his friends," Hadewijch of Antwerp writes to a young religious in the thirteenth century, "putting them to the test and complaining of their faithlessness. . . ." She has a blunt answer and a useful one for this vexed situation:

> What does it matter to us, if our intention is good and we want to exalt our lives to God, who is so great and so exalted, whether people are faithful or unfaithful to us, kind or unkind, treat us ill or well? If we cannot show good faith and kindness to them, we are harming ourselves, and the worst of the harm is that we are ruining for ourselves the sweetness of true love.

It may be painful to have to endure faithless friends. It may make us untrusting. All the more important to "confide yourself to His love"; if you do, you "will soon grow to your full stature, but if you persist in doubting, you will become sluggish and everything which you ought to do will be a burden to you." This does not call for superhuman strength. What it asks is love, offered it is true with some zeal and fervor, but that is always the requirement of love, whatever its object, human or divine. A pallid love is no love at all.[11]

But how do we develop a love that is fervid and zealous, which is to say passionate, for what we cannot see or hear or touch? It is hard enough to love what one sees, hears, tastes, touches, smells with such intensity, to really love, not simply to reach out to satisfy one's appetites. The counsel comes, simple, clear, to the point, again from an ancient text. Richard of St. Victor, master of the contemplative life of the twelfth century, says "think through the imagination," since however much one may want "to consider incorporeal things," one "dreams of the images of corporeal things only." And the Victorine offers a bold reading of scripture to reinforce his point, even, we might say, a scandalous one.

> Let the mind think through the imagination since it cannot yet by pure intelligence. This is, I think, why Rachel first had children through her handmaid before she gave birth herself; for it is sweet for her to think upon them through the imagination when she cannot yet have an intelligent understanding by the reason. As we mean reason by Rachel, so we mean the imagination by her handmaid. Therefore the reason persuades us that it is better to think about the good things in some way or other and at least to kindle the soul with desire for them through imagining their beauty, rather than to fix the mind upon false and deceptive goods. And this is the reason why Rachel wished to give her handmaid to her husband.[12]

The logic of love is scandalous for it lets nothing stand in the way of the desired object. Love hurls itself toward intimacy, and never more so than when it moves toward God. The imagination works overtime. It fixes on the paradoxes that define the most extreme loves. We lose ourselves to find ourselves. Our life apart from the other no longer means very much. It is unthinkable to live alone. We are most ourselves now when we are utterly caught up in the other. When the other is the ultimate Other and it comes to live in us, we have gone as far as the imagination can carry us. We are now in the world and condition and exquisite understanding of what Richard of St. Victor calls the pure intelligence.

The knowledge that comes this way is a living knowledge. It moves into us, it becomes us. We move into it, we become it. It is not that we identify with it, as we often do when we adopt a cause, even if we do so with the greatest fervor and zeal. This is not to take a moral stand. This is not the determination to right a wrong or effect a great change for the better. Those things may come with it, but they are not the living knowledge of love. We must not confuse love, either for the human person or the divine, with ideology and we should be able to depend upon our counselors and preachers and teachers to know this and help us to know it.

The love that inhabits us and which we inhabit in that curious indwelling that seems to defy rational process moves in its own climate, assumes its own postures and gestures, arises in astonishing ways. What is most remarkable about them, perhaps, is that they are both predictable and unpredictable. The movements are the movements of prayer; that is predictable. But they are not simply a reaching out to comfort oneself, to claim the love for oneself, nor are the words or the understanding of them what one would have thought them to be; none of that is predictable.

There is a tutelary example in the experience of Andrei Sinyavsky on his way to prison in Soviet Russia that is paradigmatic for this species of love. It is consoling for the writer, the dissident, the unfairly accused. It takes him far inside himself and far outside.

> You pray to the Mother of God when they bring you in for questioning. Hail Mary, Mother of God, blessed art Thou, the Lord is with Thee. . . . When walking down those corridors, I often asked myself: Why does the soul unfailingly, inaudibly, and unforeseeably pour itself out in prayer to the Holy Mother of God? After all, you're not asking for anything. No, of course, you do ask for something, but it's no longer for yourself.

Others are at liberty. Will they be caught?

> If things keep up like this, everyone, down to the last man, the entire human race, will be drawn into that

> hellish machine and pulped. Spare the others, O Lord! Thou who wast born as the Saviour of our souls. . . . Will worse come to worst and all humankind be under their total control?! But they can't get to Her! The Mother of God will alone remain our witness and our advocate in heaven. Hail, Immaculate Virgin! Beyond enemy reach. May She alone be saved and shine forth, the Queen of Heaven! . . . That brings some relief. Which means that even we sinners here on earth do not cackle in vain. . . .

Why, Sinyavsky asked himself, does one pray to the Mother of God? And we second the question. This splendid writer, who grew up in a household festooned with the pictures of the Soviet pantheon—Marx, Lenin, Stalin—and who is not a religious man in the ordinary sense of the term but a brilliant ironist, asks himself with each experience, "Why to the Mother of God? Not to God, not even to Christ, but to the heavenly Mother?" His answer, which is that there is no answer, is the response of love.

> I could find no answer, and we don't need any answers. A person needn't know why he's attracted to one form of supplication rather than another. Trust. Be calm. Our souls are so much more intelligent and infinite than we are. . . .[13]

Tough-minded, straightforward, clear, the counsel is love. "Confide yourself to His love," says Hadewijch of Antwerp. "Think through the imagination," says Richard of St. Victor, "think about the good things in some way or other. . . ." Andrei Sinyavsky sends us, as he sent himself, to the root meaning of faith, which is the substance of love: "Trust. Be calm. Our souls are so much more intelligent and infinite than we are. . . ."

Love, of course, is our great resource, if we are lucky enough to be graced by it, for it has the power to unite our disparate parts, to contract or reconstruct our self as we find ourselves meeting another self. A lover knows us with a pitiless lucidity and a generous appreciation. A lover is like a young child in the boundless flow of good will and love that pours out to us regardless of the hurts that we have dealt, whether we have meant to hurt or not. Aggressions get rearranged in a trusting intimacy. We fight through to the best truth of each other and what we find we find together and fight together rather than each against the other. Of course, the physical components of love are marvelous. They may be all that can match the wide openness of one body to another that we know as infants with our mothers. Such love, in body as well as soul, in mind as well as heart, will set up a humming that resounds with a simple happiness in being. Needless to say, in any relation of love—between friends, between parent and child, between lovers—laughter provides a rich feeding. Laughter arrives as a gift for which we only give thanks. And laughter, like love, must be spent at once. There is no backlog in love or laughter. It increases by being shared, by being spread abroad, by inviting all to join us at the table.

Finally, then, we may find our shelter and protection from both burnout and burn-up just by asking ourselves directly, What then do you love? Whom do you love? What makes you feel alive, real, loving, loved? What links knit themselves imaginatively over the gaps? To what, to whom, do you feel summoned? Where does the infinite meet you, where do you know being itself beyond argument? We know again, in the questions and in the answers, that ultimate truth comes from deep inside us and from far outside.

Chapter 7

Prayer and Politics

Imagination is at its most surprising in the realms of prayer and politics. In the normal order of things, these realms are sharply differentiated from each other, even opposed, as feminine and masculine so often are, or the individual and society, or the church and the world. But imagination opposes this sort of facile making of oppositions. Prayer and politics are not in fact opposed in their essential being. They complete each other. They either go together or do not meet at all. Lose one and the other skews into distortion. Our century displays only too much of the skewing. But recent events show us how much still remains of the graced pairing of prayer and politics. The recovery of the feminine modes of being from gross neglect has introduced a renewal and reform of the masculine whenever it has been strongly felt, in the countries of eastern Europe, for example, in the arts, in religion.[1]

Imagination inspires a new way of seeing, through reconciliation. It weaves links between opposites, recalling wholeness where earlier only opposing forces had seemed to exist. We really cannot live one without the other, men and women, east and west, prayer and politics. If we insist, as we have so often in the past, on seeing these oppositions as fixed and irreparable, we just prolong and intensify the divisions. Instead of healing and reconciliation, we condemn ourselves to endless strife. We accept the polarization of the sexes and the pillaging of nature and of whole peoples as inevitable. We sit by calmly as nations and cultures are all but obliterated, in the Baltic, the Balkan, the Trans-Caucasus for example. Only a defunct imagination of one in thrall to a despotic politics can produce cases with such destruction and desolation.

Imagination contemplates very different goals and procedures. It dreams up an end to unnatural division and opposition, to Berlin Walls and Securitates, whether in the politics of countries of the psyche or the spirit. No violent disunion is fixed forever in its place for the imagination. Any tyranny or sickness or depredation of the spirit or the psyche can be conquered. Karl Menninger, speaking from great experience, said that in the treatment of psychotic persons we need not just new drugs but new hope. Hope arises through the expectations of a person not just to get over a mental illness but to become "weller than well."[2] Hope displays itself in preventive action with whole communities, not just individual persons, by making many small places where city-bound people can rest from the strains of urban living, can relax, and can know together an imaginative release from stress. New York City's tiny vest-pocket parks provide such healing moments. Imagine being on a Manhattan street on a hot summer day, feet aching from walking on hard concrete, ears racked by auto horns and people yelling, eyes burning from the gasoline-filled air. Suddenly, tucked between two buildings, the width only of a narrow brownstone, we come upon a park. Water cascades down a back garden wall, bringing immediate change of atmosphere. Unobtrusive concessionaires sell soft drinks, hot dogs, or brownies. We sit in comfortable chairs, beside trees and flowers, and restore our souls. Hope incarnates in this little way. Contemplation arises in a city of convulsive action, each making the other possible, softening the unimaginative insistence on opposition—the spiritualism that counsels us to withdraw from the world as if it were damned, the activism that submerges us forever in the racket of the world.

Imagination connects. It looks to heal conflict, as so impressively it has done in bringing together the modes of feminine and masculine that for so long seemed irremediably separated and for so many still seem to be. In some businesses and professions, imaginative work-schedules have made it possible for a woman who is also a wife and mother to combine a working and family life. Instead of engendering splits in a woman, arousing in her feelings of guilt both toward her job and her child, and infecting the child with problems really spawned by society, we change the work schedule. A schedule is, after all, only a machinery of time, not a thing of flesh and blood. Parts of most jobs can be done at a desk at home as well as at an office, or at different times of day, not just from nine to five. The church needs to do some imaginative planning here in aid of its clergy's personal and family life. For most of the business of the church gets done in evening meetings, up to as many as four or five nights a week. This scheduling separates spouse from spouse and from children. Surely there are other ways business can be done, respecting parishioners' schedules and the home lives of its clergy.[3]

Using our imagination to rethink and refeel our understanding of the masculine and feminine modes of being can bridge the seeming gap between them. Such a procedure does not fix sexual categories in rigid definition but rather brings to our attention the differences in our similarities. It opens new ways for us to pray. We should note, for example, the strikingly gender-oriented prayer practices of so many of the mystics. There are insights here to rescue us from discouragement about our prayer life. It may be that a method did not work for us because we could not pray in its masculine style. As a case in point, see the way Thomas Merton describes mental prayer, as

> . . . something like a skyrocket. . . . the soul streaks heavenward in an act of intelligence as clear and direct as the rocket's trail of fire. Grace has released all the deepest energies of our spirit and assists us to climb to new and unsuspected heights. Nevertheless, our own faculties soon reach their limit . . . There is a point where the mind blows down its fiery trajectory as if to acknowledge its limitations. . . . But it is here that our "meditation" reaches its climax. Love again takes the initiative and the rocket explodes in a burst of sacrificial praise. Thus love flings out a hundred burning starts, acts of all kinds. . . .[4]

Aren't we getting a male's sexual experience in these words, with space technology used to describe a soul's experience of God? Wouldn't female experience yield very different images for the soul, such as a magnetic pulling toward and in, both a diffuse going soft and a gathering toward a sweet rush of release? Simone Weil writes about our desire as being the only thing that brings God's attention to us. Desire *is* attention. It summons God into our souls when we fix upon God our intent longings.[5] Our imaginations will not flinch either at the rich complexity of women praying in a masculine mode that they sometimes find they need or of men finding their way only through a feminine approach to imagery, even an adoption of feminine identification in their prayer images.

We do not approach religion neutrally. We always perceive religious symbols through a gender lens which itself reflects the psychological and cultural contexts that shape us. We should not, then, reduce our religious symbols to contextual conditioning. We must see that our ways of apprehending them inevitably reflect the influence of our gender lens. Men and women have long appropriated religious symbols differently, as the historian Caroline Walker Bynum shows. Women religious tend to respond to symbols by stressing the continuity between social and spiritual perceptions and biological experiences. They seem to emphasize paradox or synthesis rather than opposition or conflict. Men in religion tend to see symbols as inversions or reversals of power and status, underlining and emphasizing opposition and contradiction. Women tend to use symbols to express and explore states of being whereas men use them to construct stages of relationship between self and other.[6] We must recognize that these ways of approaching religious symbols are just ways of approach and not fixed attributes of the sexes. Any given person, male or female, can make use of either or both of these modalities.

Lewis Hyde directs our attention to the influence of masculine and feminine modalities in commerce and the economics of property.[7] He contrasts two dominant kinds of work, which he calls gift labor and market labor. Gift labor cannot be undertaken in a measured time, such as office hours, the conscious quantitative style of the labor market. Relationship characterizes gift labor, the focus of which is the development of the soul. Market labor is designed to produce commodities. It conducts itself on a cost-benefit basis. Gift labor involves a sense of call. It creates a vocation. It inhibits our ability to sell ourselves or our products. Gift labor yields increase and profit by disbursing gifts, not by hoarding or investing or saving up, in the mode of market labor. Gift labor spends itself freely and returns to a state of emptiness. Market labor capitalizes on its creations and does not squander. Rather, it plots its course and accepts its risks. Gift labor, in its sharing of its gifts, gathers people into cohesive and organic relationships with each other. How to engage in gift labor and permit it to survive in the organized market labor of society is a task that imagination must work on. The way market and gift labor complete each other, precisely because of their differences, parallels the way prayer and politics reach out to each other.

Gift labor reveals a kind of praying at its source. For our gift—in art or religion or our intimate lives together—rises from a source beyond our egos which we must acknowledge in order to have our gifts at our disposal to give to others. Like prayer, giving means acknowledging our own emptiness before the source of our creation. We confess that our vessel is empty without the source that fills it. Receiving, we can then give out of what we receive and out of what we have made of what we have received. We do not hoard. As Hyde says, a gift must stay in motion; that is the internal demand of the creative spirit. We do not empty the gift source by sharing it, but as when we cast our bread upon the waters, it comes back a hundredfold. There is no backlog in love. It must be spent continually, circulating, creating, connecting us into a great circle that holds us all in being. Giving the gift feels like being prayed by the prayer that moves inside us, which, we may finally come to recognize, we did not ourselves create. It is the God in us who starts us wanting to pray and to go on praying—or painting or writing or composing or, in the truest sense, making love.[8]

Prayer and the arts must be the product of gift labor or in almost every case fail to meet their object or express their subject. The work of art that is crafted simply to meet a market demand is at best an expression of craftsmanship, in which we can see the command of color or line or texture or hear a control of instrumental resources or orchestration, even a dazzling display of language, but in aid chiefly of a box-office standard. Selling is the point, not a content of substance. A musical cue is constructed with equal fervor to promote a soft drink, a detergent, or a cops-and-robbers chase. A motif is borrowed from Mondrian or Picasso or sado-masochistic pornography to make lingerie or jeans appealing, with equal lack of concern for the trivialization of high modernist art or the debasing of human sexuality. Grace—a free gift—is not the word one would choose to describe the effect of such performances, unless something escapes the eye or ear or mind-set trained on the market, and suddenly real feeling, a fine taste, a content of substance sneaks in or even leaps through, as certainly we have seen or heard or read in advertising art from time to time.

The imagination lies in wait for such moments. It is eager and ready to trap the artist or his employer with the real content of art, which is the sensibility of the artist, mediating between the experience of the outside world and the artist's interiority with the tools and materials of art. Such art-work, like all art of quality, is good for nothing. It is directed to no utilitarian purpose, and certainly not to sell goods or make a political statement or even to propagate a faith, but it may be so winning in its linking of inner and outer worlds that it ends up by selling more soft drinks or hard soap than the crassly commercial stuff. Perhaps even more startlingly, an artist who is far from what would be defined as a state of grace in theological terms may enlarge our understanding of a religious doctrine, a mystery, a saintly or a scriptural figure in ways that devout practitioners of religion all too often miss entirely.

This is where art and prayer meet. The mere recital of sacred words, no matter how well intentioned, may not get us much beyond a self-congratulatory sanctimoniousness. A garbled cry of anxiety, with few details clear except those that convey an aching uneasiness and the trust that somehow somewhere somebody will answer the cry with help, will almost always do better. That honest plumbing of the hurt is what is heard, not a smooth recital of honeyed phrases. The faith that leads to such honesty is the art of prayer. It produces a content. It reflects an ardent sensibility. It is heard.

In both cases, that of art and that of prayer, some technical skill and learning in the processes and materials of the domains will certainly not go amiss. Imagination requires support. Usually, if its presence is strong enough, it will find that support. The artist who has a strong interior vision will find what is necessary—the colors, the tones, the images, the formal structures. Henri Matisse can turn a scene of the utmost commonplaceness, tree branches seen through a window, a bowl of fruit, a neighboring curtain design, into a meeting with being itself, as rich in its communication of human presence as one of his languid odalisques stretching her arms over her nude torso or his boldly limned St. Dominic, with no details of head or face, just a great commanding figure on the white wall of an elegant little chapel.[9]

Wallace Stevens, who confessed a belief in images that assumed the proportions of a religious faith, made a poetry out of the imagination that, rather than diminishing prosaic reality, constantly enlarged it. To indulge the imagination was for him to make reality come alive, to be sensitive in new ways to the miracles of the mundane. Poetry, he said, "has to be a revelation of nature." Its power is such that it can be "a purging of the world's poverty and change and evil and death. It is a present perfecting, a satisfaction in the irremediable poverty of life." In saying such things, he is not retreating from the immeasurable difficulties of life; he is not calling us away from other solutions to our problems or the world's. He, who regularly refused to ally himself to one or another political party or position, offers instead the healing strengths of the imagination. In his finely limned poetic he is saying, like Jesus, that the poor we will always have with us, and even more, that the poor we will always be, except as we reach to the revelation with which the ordinary is charged.

Steven's prayerful truths are found in their most confident distillations, perhaps, in the little poems of the last years of his life. Driving home on a Friday night in summer, across the middle of Connecticut, from Cornwall to Hartford, he sees "not a night blown at a glassworks in Vienna or Venice, motionless, gathering time and dust," but things turning up and turning away, the "visible transformations of summer night," and he is moved to celebrate the event.

An argentine abstraction approaching form
And suddenly denying itself away.

The solidity of matter thus confronted becomes "an insolid billowing." The poem leaps and languishes in the play of the imagination, in the spirit of the summer month on which the portentous title of the poem puns, "Reality is an Activity of the Most August Imagination."

Stevens and Matisse pray for us by endowing everything around us with freshness and caprice. "Local objects," Stevens says in the poem of that name, "become More precious than the most precious objects of home"; they are "not present as a matter of course. . . ."[10] We look at things around us; we introject them like our mothers' milk. We dwell on them, pray through them, a branch at the window, a curtain design, the silver flow, the gold burst of the disappearances and appearances of objects in a car's lights on a bright August night: revelation, the rhythm of revelation.

That is the pulse of the music of Duke Ellington, a conversion in the syllables of jazz-time of everything that happens in the course of one's days into the sacred concert which with the passing of years his music became. That is to speak not only of the formal gatherings of pieces into what he called Sacred Concerts, but all the pauseful deliberate movements round feeling, such as "Reminiscing in Tempo," his first attempt at something more extended than the three-minute lyricism permitted by the ten-inch 78 rpm record to which jazz bands were confined for so many years. That is to connect the long, sometimes overlong "tone parallel to the life of the American Negro," that Duke called *Black, Brown and Beige* after the colors of his people, to the two-minute and sixteen-seconds musing on "Something Sexual" for alto saxophone and orchestra, with a couple of male vocal lines without words to punctuate the musing.

That last little piece, like Stevens' little stipplings of poems at the end of his life and Matisse's terse geometry of sanctity, haunts. It will not go away, once one has heard it. It says so much by saying so little and saying what it says with such authority. The voice we hear is assured. It is part of the Ellington choir, a perfection of jazz sound molded by years of participation in collective enterprise, with a tune contributed by Duke or by the solo instrumentalist, a ground made by the leader, on paper, at the piano, in his great striding far-reaching presence. There was always a voice for what Duke felt: Johnny Hodges's alto saxophone or Harry Carney's baritone saxophone, somebody's growling trumpet, Bubber Miley's or Cootie Williams', or a similar trombone presence, Tricky Sam Nanton's. It could be the insistent presence of two bass players, when that seemed right, or of Jimmy Blanton, whose one bass combined a solidity of matter with "an insolid billowing" that no whole section of basses in a symphony orchestra could match. It might be that odd, sometimes querulous, often wispily sexual violin of Ray Nance, doing double duty away from his crackling trumpet. There was always a ground, the one that Duke himself provided, on paper and at the piano, like the terra firma that we find in the allegorical paintings of the late middle ages and the renaissance, where the mysteries of scripture take root—nativity, visitation, passion, crucifixion, resurrection. In each case transcendence finds its home, here, among us, in the world.[11]

Madness becomes sanity in such a grounding. Poverty becomes riches and riches that we can take in and hold onto, beyond the temptations of avarice, with none of the fears of recession or inflation or of war or revolution. Think how little the greatest figures we know would seem if they were left ungrounded; yes, even the giants of the mysteries, the centers of our worship and wisdom, Jesus, Mary, Adam, Eve, Abraham, Sarah, Isaac, Elizabeth, John the Baptist, Samson, Jerome, Anthony, Teresa. It is their grounding in the recognizable things of this world that gives them their flesh. They are palpable to us because we have seen them in our midst—their midst—in landscapes, rooms, stables, deserts, country roads, city streets. They wear their clothes; they wear our clothes. They look like people we know. They are people we know.

St. Jerome, fierce-tempered, glowering, more frightening perhaps than the lion that is his invariable companion, looks up at us from a cave which may be iconographically the remnants of the crumbling old law but has the reassuring quality of looking like rocks we know, stones we may have skinned ourselves on in our games as children. St. Teresa, shoeless, open-mouthed, eyes closed or drooping at least, her whole body slack with spent fervor, may be mid-air in a Bernini relief, a distant sixteenth-century Spanish mystic suspended on a Roman church wall, but her bodily attitude is altogether familiar to anyone past pubescence. The passion she has given to God is drawn from the voluptuary treasure-house with which we are all endowed. We may not have given such feeling to man or God, but we know about it; we have felt enough of it to recognize it; we are grounded.[12]

This art of the saints of the imagination—painters, sculptors, poets, musicians—is in one sense really good for nothing. Like the imagination to which it is dedicated, it has no immediate negotiable value. It may tune our perceptions to a finer edge. It may warm our devotions. It may make us look around, listen, taste, touch, smell with new awareness. But such art, like our prayers for surcease from all pain and suffering or for sudden fame, a movie contract, instant recognition in the streets, untold wealth, will not quickly, unmistakably, gloriously change our lives. Only we can do that by what we bring to our art and to our prayers that will permit us to take away from our art and our prayers what is really there, namely ourselves.

Being is what we come to with such a labor of giving and being is the mode in which we come to it. Not only finally, in any summary moment of our lives after birth, but in each little moment in which we claim our being, we find the rewards of being. We know, through good-for-nothing art and speak-for-everything prayer, the modalities of possibility that our being men or women brings us, if we are fully willing to be men or women and accept the femininity and masculinity that come with that willingness. It is not a simple acceptance. It does not reduce us to a one-dimensional fixed maleness or femaleness. It makes us womanly with a calm acceptance of whatever masculine elements course through our female being. It makes us manly with an easy assurance in the feminine graces that may turn up in our working imagination. We find a healing strength and wholeness in living with such range and contrast.

The contrast between the feminine and masculine modes of being human, which belong to all of us, men and women alike, figures in all the ancient stories. It has to do with how societies position themselves in relation to the center of their social being. The hero's way, exemplifying the masculine mode, is to set out to accomplish a goal, or as in some story-endings, to renounce the goal, feeling he has failed and may even have to abandon the heroic role forever. The feminine approach shows a different departure point, one that the Percival of the Grail legend had to learn. He finally learned to ask the right question of the Grail, a feminine symbol of centeredness, and to ask what was lacking that resulted in the old Fisher King suffering a mortal wound. The feminine approach involves positioning ourself toward the center. Asking is the mode here. We open our inquiry with a deliberate not-knowing, rather than defining our goal as if we really knew it and going straight at it. We relate to the center by serving—the point is to see whom the Grail serves —rather than by acquiring the Grail as so much bankable treasure. The contrast and opposition of success and failure, between achieving heroic stature and abandoning it, are muted in this approach. Rather, we look at things from the Grail's point of view, so to speak.

The feminine mode is maddening to us when we approach it through an over-determined, over-emphasized masculine perspective. It must seem ephemeral, elusive, impractical. It never defines itself or offers a clear, concise definition of its "position." And that is true to its mode. The feminine does not launch a program, list a curriculum, or give a list of do's and don't's. It has little to say about "rights." In board meetings of institutions, for example, a person speaking out of the feminine mode is apt to ask about the spirit in which the whole institution conducts its business, a question that may seem contentious or time-wasting to those who want to get down to cases and vote on proposals in front of them. But in the long run this is the question that proves most practical, because decisions to act made from the wrong premises usually cause great harm or, at best, just move things around in place. The "position paper" of the feminine approach is always to position itself toward the center, to identify what really matters, and to let doing flow from that central connection to being. It is concerned with a stringent particularity, so that, for example, political options are always considered from the point of view of what fosters a person's growth and what nullifies it.

The failure of Communist theorists and rulers to understand the issues of identity and spirit which go with the feminine position have much to do with the collapse of Communist states. The conventional wisdom is that economic crisis brought East Germany, Czechoslovakia, Poland, Rumania, Bulgaria, Yugoslavia, and Hungary to their knees, but that is simply to repeat the simplistic reductionism of the so-called Marxist-Leninist position, which has almost everywhere proved weak, stumbling, out of date. Yes, the failure of the Iron Curtain countries and Soviet Russia and Communist China to provide consumer goods to their peoples has certainly had much to do with the great outburst of disgust by those peoples, the marches in defiance, in protest, in derision. But no, instrumental as the wretched economic life in these countries has been in fomenting discord, there has been something more important, which accounts for the volume of the protest, the solemnity of the protesters, the unmistakable substance of their position.

What the Communist leaders have simply not understood is the cries for identity, or the full-throated demands of the spirit. It is not just ancient hatreds that pit Azerbaijanis against Armenians, nor is it just a capricious revival of Baltic or Balkan chauvinisms that motivates the defections from the Party and the multinational states in Lithuania, Estonia, and Latvia, in Montenegro, Slovenia, Macedonia, and the rest of those pocket states of the Yugoslavian peninsula. This is an unseating by something approaching spontaneous combustion of the emptiness from above that has everywhere in the Communist world met the imaginative stirrings of the people from below. This is the fire this time, not next time.

Stalin used to speak with a great rhetorical flourish of the self-determination of all the subject peoples who made up the Union of Socialist Soviet Republics. What that meant in practice was a certain amount of folk singing and dancing and pandering to the most egregious ethnicity through native costumes and publications of a studied banality in the old languages of these peoples. Authority—political, social, economic, literary, religious, cultural—remained in Russian hands. The need to give voice to feelings and convictions, faiths and dreams altogether unprovided for in the Marxist-Leninist devotions was just not understood by the Kremlin or its satrapies. Neither regional companies of singers and dancers, at one extreme, nor gulags at the other could take care of the problem. It was too large, too complex; it reached too far, with too much imagination, into issues of personal growth and community spirit; it came too quickly and too firmly to the things that really matter to be dealt with by the Marxist-Leninist *nomenklatura*, perhaps the lowest form the bureaucratic mind has ever assumed. One has only to see how utterly without grace the Soviet rulers and their strutting henchmen were in the realms of the imagination to understand the events of 1989 and 1990, more important in their way, more revolutionary, more assertive of the worth of the human than any of the celebrated violences of 1789 and 1905 and 1917 or the declarations that accompanied them.

In the USSR, Lysenkoism declared against all the evidence that acquired traits could be, must be inherited. Scientists of distinction—and probity and courage—who demonstrated, or after awhile even attempted to demonstrate, the ludicrousness, the shamefulness, the danger to scientific truth of Lysenko and his theories lost their authority, lost their positions, and some of them even their lives. Truth became what the dictators declared it to be. It was not only world domination that the Communist dictatorship of the proletariat aimed at, but the conquest of the psyche and the spirit. And such was the weakness of the imagination of the dictators that they really believed they could do it. They came themselves to believe that if one developed a positive quality in one generation—a mathematical skill, a proficiency in playing a musical instrument, a cow that gave more milk, a richer wheat and an accompanying increase of production—it would be inherited by the next generation. But in fact mathematicians did not invariably pass on their quickness of mind, or violin and piano virtuosi necessarily give birth to prodigies, and the cows and the wheat proved particularly recalcitrant. Without any evident shame, they produced less, grew smaller, simply refused to do as Lysenko and Stalin commanded.[13]

The situation is described in chilling words by Vaclav Havel, the playwright-dissident who became the first president of the Czechoslovakia of the imagination that replaced the Czechoslovakia of despair at the end of 1989. In his first speech, he described a turning away from the "enormous creative and spiritual potential" of his country, an "obsolete economy . . . wasting the little energy we have available," a country that in education "ranks . . . 72nd in the world." He speaks of polluted earth, rivers, forests, or rulers who "for decades . . . did not look out of the windows of their aeroplanes." But as he says, "all this is still not the main problem. The worst thing is that we live in a contaminated moral environment." The words that follow are simple, straightforward, and eloquent in describing the diseased imagination of totalitarianism.

> We felt morally ill because we became used to saying something different from what we thought. We learned not to believe in anything, to ignore each other, to care only about ourselves. Concepts such as love, friendship, compassion, humility or forgiveness lost their depth and dimensions and for many of us they represented only psychological peculiarities, or they resembled gone astray greetings from ancient times, a little ridiculous in the era of computers and spaceships.[14]

Havel, a professional of the imagination, knows its healing powers and can speak to them with particular authority. But even those without the acquired traits make the same points about life under Ceausescu in Rumania, under all the tsars of Communism in Russia, from Lenin to Gorbachev, wherever the extravagant promises of the workers' utopia have been spelled out in exact detail and utterly unfulfilled with the same precision, promise for promise, failure for failure. The promises were always precisely defined, in one five-year plan after another.

The failures were always complete, in one five-year plan after another. Nothing was left to the imagination. There was never anything that could be reproached for a feminine inexactness.

In terms of symbolic analysis, the feminine mode describes an approach linking us up, bringing us near, putting us in the midst of matters at hand rather than the standing back, observing, and grasping things through definitive descriptions so characteristic of the masculine mode. The feminine is not normally drawn toward new programs or new jargons but rather toward ways of perceiving and apperceiving, of articulating the indefinable but strongly felt connectedness between us and others, between us and matters at hand, between us and those who have lived before us and those who will live after.[15] In this approach we are caught by the particular and the special. Only that way can we reach the universal and the general. It is always the concrete person before the abstract principle. The feminine has to do with identification, a knowing by sharing a sense of being with another. Doing means doing for. This is an embodied knowing, a knowing in blood and bone, in particular groups and places, in the times and cultures of which we are a part. We reach differentiation through the samenesses we share more than through the differences that set us apart. We reach clarity through analogy rather than contrast. Miss Marple, Agatha Christie's aged sleuth, solved all her crimes from the ground up, from the unconscious leading her toward consciousness. She saw resemblances in character between a suspect and someone she knew in her little village. A character resembled a girl Miss Marple had trained as a maid, for example. Though she was markedly different in her station and her presentation of self, she nonetheless harbored the same lazy little habits and fierce graspings out of envy of the girl Miss Marple had trained. Thus it was possible to conceive this character as a murderer.

In contrast to such procedure, the masculine mode of being relates by differentiation. It knows by knowing about. It does by doing to or toward. Here we know both our separateness from and our possibilities of relationship to a thou and an other. We can abstract from detail and formulate precise definitions that cover all particular instances of a universal phenomenon, in contrast to that mode that proceeds by example rather than definition, the feminine one. Think of the images the gospel thrusts at us, such as the woman who would not take no for an answer but insisted she get at least some crumbs from the Lord's table. We repeat her act in every eucharist when we pray "we are not worthy to gather up the crumbs from under thy table. . . ." Think, too, of the woman who stole a healing touch from Jesus when he was surrounded by throngs of people. Theft, nothing less. She took her healing moment in secret, to be exposed only by Jesus's question: Who touched me? What could she say in her defense? I had to have it? I needed it so much? Imagine all her fervor for God's touch! What would it mean for us to be that greedy and grabbing in our desire for God?

We have heard a lot in recent years about what is wrong with the masculine mode of being when the feminine mode is neglected or rejected. What about the masculine when the feminine is accepted and honored? What happens then? What does the masculine look like from the point of view of the well-received and receiving feminine? It looks like an indefinable spirit which does not preach or hector but brings a truth by which we can live and for the sake of which we will interrupt our fixed routines of sleeping, eating, resting, working. We want to hear, to perceive, and more, to acquire this different departure-point. The masculine initiates change by not only demanding but actually compelling new directions.[16] It can pounce and make us want to pounce and take on different ways. It moves us into strong new relationships with others who nonetheless retain their separateness, distinctly themselves even when we engage them intimately. We do not merge or fuse or totally identify with them. Rather we meet and salute them and their differences. We confront differences with our own point of view. The masculine, we see, spans heaven and earth in its own characteristic ways. As chthonic energy it pushes up from the depths like Poseidon's horses leaping from the sea. Passionate in its pushing, this energy pokes into and presses past given limits. It also comes as if from above, like lightning bolts from Zeus, or like Yahweh's voice speaking out of the desert, telling us to leave everything we know and journey to a new land. The masculine word sends something new into our midst, and calls us into fearsome places to identify what tempts us and choose what to give ourselves to.

Just as our imagination shows us that the masculine and feminine are not warring opposites but operate in all of us, men and women both, and together give us access to a more complete life, so too it shows the secret links between other pairs of opposites. A particularly pernicious opposition identifies the social life we share together as the enemy of our individual fulfillment, though in fact each badly needs the other just to exist.

Loss of imagination leads to social and individual crime. Children deprived of play fail to construct a capacity to construct a map either of themselves or of their boundaries. They do not develop the capacity to plan activities in sequence or carry them out in action. Instead, dangerously fluid space, disconnected time, fragments of "me" in "you" and "you" in "me" explode in the child. Everything calls for immediacy. And so we have teenage and adult citizens who cannot postpone gratification, who suddenly must "go off," who "go wild" with anger against anyone who seems to stand in their way. They wreck their own lives and those of almost everyone around them.[17]

Deprivation of play is a privation of being we all know. It observes no boundary of social or economic class.[18] The mother exhausted from working all day, in a ceaseless battle against poverty, sits apathetically, passively holding her infant with little interaction or even distinguishable facial expression for her baby to see and internalize. The wealthy mother who heaps her infant with toys but does not take the time to play with the child produces the same privation. People who use their imagination here understand that they are not compelled to act but are able to choose when and where and how to act or not to act. The negative examples make the point. The papers reported the story of a man who could not use his imagination to heal his overwhelming sense of outrage and ruined his own life and that of another. He was driving his new car in New York City traffic. Another driver wanted to inch up alongside him, to position himself at a light in order to burst forth ahead of others waiting there. When the light changed from red to green, he dashed ahead, much too close to the new car. He scratched the shining new paint all along one side from rear to front. The first man heard the terrible scratching noise. He jumped out and saw what had happened. Enraged, he followed the culprit to the next light, took a gun from his glove compartment, went up to the driver's window and shot him dead. He didn't stop to imagine what other things could be done, as he had never stopped to imagine the possible consequences of carrying a gun in a car. Impulse without an instructing imagination equalled murder. No matter where we come down in gun-control arguments, we must use our imaginations, whether to control crime, prevent it, or punish it.

Imagination about what tortures one would want to inflict on the culprit who scratches our shiny new car is a way actually to contain our rage while gaining time against impulsive action. Without imagination, one man's life was over and the other's ruined. As Bruno Bettelheim puts it, violence is the behavior of someone who cannot imagine any other solution to a besetting problem.[19] Imagination must enter here. We must ask how violence can be discharged in ways that are socially useful. The wish to understand and master what is threatening to us can be a powerful motivation for learning. In imagination we can identify the urgent need for simple recognition as persons. We all feel so desperate when we are trapped in interminable lines waiting for automobile-license forms, at airline check-in counters, at the post office, at the bank, or the state unemployment office. When we finally reach our turn and ask questions about forms and procedures, it doesn't matter whether we are treated with soothing noises or angry responses, it is clear that we do not matter and are just to be gotten rid of, one way or another. Then we feel our very being is threatened. Bureaucratic procedure is a monument to failed imagination.

Bettelheim, like a whole series of wise people reaching back to the Italian renaissance, urges us to use imagination to remember persons in planning city buildings.[20] Social spaces need to be extensions of private space. We need playgrounds small enough to hear conversation and buildings near enough for parents to see their children in the playground. When children feel safe they can make a public space their own. One mother accompanied her child to the play space of her building for a longer period than most parents do. When she was dismissed by her son finally as not needed, it was because her little boy had imaginatively taken possession of the entire space as his own. He would call out to newcomers, greeting them as if they had entered his home, and so they had. If a building is so high it dwarfs persons, or corridors are so long and thin one feels like an insect in a great hive, the building creates anger rather than living space. As we see in cities with huge budgets to clean off graffiti, young males will assert their virile personhood by writing all over such buildings or the equivalent, subway cars, at least in part to rid themselves of feeling dwarfed.

We need to use our imagination in addressing the homeless. Are they escaping from a crushing anonymity to a self-created space, even if it is only a cardboard shelter in a city park? Some citizens see this and respond by opening small homeless shelters, seeing even well-provided large places as part of the problem. Seeing the life of psyche and soul as a part of each person, a task not beyond anyone's power of imagination, brings healing. The psychiatrist Harry Wilmer treated Vietnam veterans suffering post-traumatic stress disorder by constructing small communities to pay attention to their nightmares, visitations that would come two or three times a night and prevent them for over a decade from gaining a full night's sleep. In these communities which became dream circles, each man in turn would tell his nightmare in detail, repeating and repeating it as it repeated itself in his dreams. The others would listen and pay attention and pay respect, no matter how often the story was repeated. Gradually, over months, the traumatic dream would begin to vary in very small details, indicating that the dreamer's psyche was at last beginning to absorb and make use of the deep shock to his soul.[21]

The diaries and letters of Etty Hillesum, written in Nazi deportation camps, show us how imagination can sustain us even in the most intense anguish, after seeing our country overrun, our friends carted off like so much refuse, our whole life crushed by brutal indifference.[22] For the impresarios of the Holocaust, there were no individual psyches or souls. But of course there were, not only in the victims, but in their victimizers. Neglect of imagination, that great maker of sanity in psyche and soul, can produce what is not so lightly called unimaginable horror. As Jung puts it

> . . . the careful consideration of psychic factors is of importance in restoring not merely the individual's balance but society's as well, otherwise the destructive tendencies easily gain the upper hand. In the same way as the atom bomb is an unparalleled means of physical mass destruction, so the misguided development of the soul must lead to mass destruction.[23]

Etty Hillesum found her balance through an unexpected rising of a mystical gift. In the midst of the terror dwelt religious tasks.

> It is the hatred of our age: hatred of the Germans poisons everyone's mind. . . . If there were one decent German, then he should be cherished despite the whole barbaric gang, and because of that one decent German it is wrong to pour hatred over an entire people. . . . It is sickness of the soul. Socialism lets in hatred against everything that is not socialist through the back door. . . . German soldiers suffer as well. There are no frontiers between suffering people, and we must pray for them all.[24]

In this urge to pray that she felt so strongly there at the center of evil in her time, Hillesum found new theological vision. We must take care of God and then nothing can touch us. "The surface of the earth is turning into one great prison camp and soon there will be nobody left outside. . . ." But inside the prison, there was something to do. It was clear, she reasoned,

> that You God cannot help us, that we must help you to help ourselves . . . and that is all that matters. . . . You cannot help us but we must help you and defend your dwelling place inside us to the last . . . no one is in their clutches who is in your arms. . . . I shall never drive you from my presence.[25]

Hillesum embodies the begetting energy of both psyche and soul that imagination brings into play, and nowhere more powerfully than in prayer. We see another of our pairs of opposites dissipated in the secret link we discover between action and contemplation. In any enduring prayer life, we are drawn both to act and to contemplate. With luck and grace and perseverance, we can reach their integration in what has been called contemplation in action.[26]

A central mark of religious experience is the accompanying urge to step over into visible life; it insists on being experienced. That is the point of incarnation. Not only is that the way prayer functions psychologically, it is the way it functions socially. When we pray to God to confess something or just simply to bring before our imaginative eye what occupies and preoccupies our days, we become conscious of our most burdensome anxieties and thus keep known sufferings from turning into unknown ones. For even when they disappear into the unconscious, they will quickly enough reappear in anti-social behavior or psychosomatic symptoms and complications. As the psychoanalyst Masud Khan points out, if we cannot live in our dream space, it will move over to invade our social space.[27] The horror of the transmutation of a quiet, retiring man into a paranoid sniper, shooting down innocent victims in a MacDonald's restaurant because he thinks "they" are out to get him, shows the power of the imagination run amok.

Imagination provides the primary space for our inner life. If we cannot use it to house all of the psyche, the shadowy bad as well as the unmistakably good, the bitter transformation will occur and we will make our contribution to the world's evils, social, political, whatever. Imprisonment in our rigid defenses will force us to look for a form of government to imprison even more of us in its totalitarian embrace. Our unhappiness in our own bodies will make us want to visit a matching misery upon other people's bodies, instilling even in our own children fear of and contempt for instinctual life. Our own ill health makes us envy others' good health. Our lack of love makes us want to spoil their loving relationships. Suffering from the loss of freedom to depression or anxiety, we seek to destroy others' freedom.[28] The life of the spirit, and especially prayer, where we can unburden our agony, may keep us from infecting our neighbors, or if we are healthy enough, will allow us to carry the guilt the inequities of the world too often entail and make something positive of it.

Contemplation of the world's imbalances does not lead us to escape from the world, but to positive ways of action in the world. Urs von Balthasar shrewdly sums up the social effect of contemplation: "Contemplatives are like great subterranean rivers, which, on occasion, break out into springs at unexpected points, or reveal their presence only by the plants they feed from below."[29] In praying we are brought in touch with the powerful love of God who seeks out a dedicated people in Israel, or comes to us in person as Jesus Christ. Incarnation requires the world. Prayer without action is like a voice without a supporting body. And action without prayer is like a body without a voice.

Action in contemplation involves a suppleness of imagination which allows us almost to assume the being of others while simultaneously remaining ourselves. We see, we participate, we enter into the other whose being still exists in its own right. We surrender to our spontaneous responses, whatever they are, without self-consciousness. At the same time we stand aside from both these sets of operations. We are both caught up in receiving the being of others into our own, and in identifying our burgeoning responses to what stands there before us, and miraculously at the same time we disidentify with our images. We have them but they do not have us.[30]

We need all our aggression to keep in touch with and make good use of all this imaginative reception and identification, this simultaneous holding onto and letting go. Out of it will come new actions, even if we do not quite know from where. All of us, to take a clear example, have strong reactions to the homeless who roam our streets. We run the gamut of feelings from compassion to anger. Looking, seeing, letting be what our imagination presents to us, reflecting at prayerful length on what we behold, can lead to new and fresh possibilities for action. Are these homeless persons acting out the loss of transcendence in our world? Are they showing us how serious the loss is of that firm connection to our sexual identity that the feminine mode of approach initiates, all so crudely lifted from us and replaced by the welfare state? Here are people with no place to lay their heads, no bathrooms, nowhere to bathe, utterly dissociated from the reigning culture. They expose to us the overdoing of our culture, and especially its tyrannical schedules of worldly accomplishment where even exercise becomes something to achieve in the world. The homeless person acts out the opposite —an endless unscheduled time, a consciousness divorced from expediency.

Some of the homeless suffer from the psychological condition called "borderline" that has become the focus of increasing investigation and speculation in the last decade.[31] Here the ego is not whole or functional, as it is meant to be, like a bit of cohesive and solid earth rescued from the sea of unconsciousness. Instead the ego presents itself more as an archipelago, a string of islands half immersed in the sea. What is maddening about such a psychic constellation brought to treatment is that when the analyst comes to meet the client on one island, the client will hop right off to the next island. Every Yes is met by an opposing No. Only a very large vision can encompass all the islands and see that the borderline person's infamous negativity may also symbolize a spiritual perception. No one view of the whole can be correct. Because of our finiteness, all our views can only convey part of the story, reveal only one or two of the many islands. The pathology of the borderline condition forces on us a healthy perception—that the transcendent can break through anywhere, in-between or right upon any of our islands, and that clearly all of us live on only one or two islands of consciousness at a time and must never take our partial view for the whole.

Much political strife issues from mistaking a partial, one-island view for the whole and insisting that everyone else must adopt it too. Imagination reminds us that we have only bits of the truth at our disposal and at best can bring those bits together into a mosaic of a partial good, but never the perfect good or the whole truth. To accept the gap between our occluded vision and the full truth energizes political action while at the same time reminding us that any action can only be partly effective. We need to exercise our imaginations before labor comes to a halt, before mines cave in, before hostages are taken, before terrorists strike. We must imagine our way into other person's shoes and try to see what the problem and its possible solutions look like to them, and equally where we and they may be tempted to precipitous action. Imagination may even return us to the true nature of religion and the church.

A church community is formed by consciousness of God coming down into our midst. It conforms, in psychological terms, to symbols of transcendence, not to ends altogether immanent in its humanity or utilitarian purposes. A Christian church community can have no merely utilitarian end. It is not principally an agent of change, a mental-health center, a problem solver, or even a builder of community. Its defining function is to worship the trinitarian God in Christ.[32] Worship is everything and nothing; its goodness is good for nothing. We choose to enter a reality, to see at some deep level that we belong to the God who made us and still makes us, who suffered and died to bring us home. The church accords reverence to the god-images in our midst that point unmistakably to God. That is what prayer is about and what must underlie political communities concerned with immanent ends and expedient action. When politics is divorced entirely from prayer, it risks becoming inflated with the substitutes for the transcendent which it confuses with the real thing. We have seen the major symptom of that inflation many times in our century—the fruitless, despotic, unbending seeking of utopia on earth, a utopia quickly turned dystopia, creating a society lethal to its citizens and utterly intolerant of opposing points of view.

The figure of Sophia personifies the anti-utilitarian,

worship-centered church. This wisdom figure, this female voice in scripture, this otherwise nameless "I am," neither god nor goddess, evokes all our unconscious experiences of the divine. She sets up her table in the marketplace, bringing God into our midst, showing us God's passionate love for us. Sophia is that spirit of imagination that engenders in us a creative living which is a living in God. It has sometimes been identified with Jesus, but it has never been pinned down, equated with anything precisely or defined beyond question. She, this elusive feminine figure, is what hovers over all our great gaps of understanding. She emboldens us to empty our preconceived notions of what should be, to let be the most embarrassing images that come to us, to look at them and to do something with them which we can then offer to others. How else could so many men and women find the courage to get up as preachers Sunday after Sunday and speak their own thoughts about the divine to their waiting congregations? Sophia symbolizes the mysterious circling back of the graces of faith to their source. We receive its bestowal by emptying out our knowing better and by returning to others what we receive from the source. That bestowal on our part leaves us empty to receive those graces again. Accepting our inner poverty, we know the richest of riches.

Chapter 8

Resurrection

We all know that imagination lives and shapes our persons, making objective reality alive and interesting to us because of our imaginings about it.[1] We know imagination as it operates among us socially and politically, sometimes fearfully, as persecutions leap from fantasy into violent reality. We are not as aware as we might be of the extent to which imagination addresses us spiritually. Across the wide gaps between all we sense of God and the pictures our religious traditions give us, our imagination plays. It weaves connections between our very personal god-images and our cultural and official ones, as we renew religious tradition with our living experience, and contain and enlarge our living experience within the great words and images of tradition. Out of this imaginative meeting across the gap emerges a spiritual experience that is alive, unmistakably real, very much our own and yet remains strongly shaped by tradition.

Still, for all that, we know that our pictures of God, personal or traditional, do not equate with God.[2] The unfathomable mystery of deity abides. Even what we may call the archetypal core of our pictures cannot be equated with God, though they reveal much in their odd way. Some pictures, like that of the priest who suddenly was visited by God as a great big Mama seated in a swivel chair in front of a television set, tuning in all her children, link up with Lady Julian's fourteenth-century "showing" of the God who is Wisdom as our mother, and Jesus too as the mother bearing us into the new life of the spirit.[3] There are primordial truths in such non-reductive mother images. For others the archetypal God is a mysterious self-giving father, who gives us not a product or an abstraction, like redemption, but his own flesh and blood, his son, who is both himself and his utmost love. Archetypal images act as lenses to refract our experience of the numinous primordium.

Our religious imaginations press the question as far as it will go. Though we honor the different primordial lenses through which the invisible becomes visible in different ways to different people, we cannot say it does not matter which lens we use, that all these pictures are relative to person or group or context, that one will serve as well as another. There are two reasons to say that will not do. The first is that such an attitude is too careless about God. When God comes to us, it matters very much how and to whom and in what form and where. A hallmark of religious experience is its specificity, even to the exact time and date as illustrated in Pascal's famous *Mémorial*. He described the exact moment, date, time of night, and all the associations, and never lost contact with it, keeping his record of the event pinned to his shirt for all his succeeding days.[4] There is nothing vague or general about such an event. It is concrete, particular. It rips time in two. Thenceforth everything is marked as before or after. It is our central date and moment. We gain our history from it. And our subsequent imaginings about the experience arrive in specific images that order not only our inner history, but all our shared history with others, delineating all we know as community.[5]

The second reason a loose relativism about god-images will not do is that it ignores the reality of the imagination. Imagining is always rooted in the body, in time, in history. We make use of our instincts, of our active experiences, of the languages native to our own particular culture. We depend on specific traditions in literature, the visual arts, music, dance, the theater, and film to express this new happening. We are finite and particular and must use what is most immediately available to us, something that at once nullifies and fulfills tradition. We cannot shop among endless options to discover the right word or image to express the coming of God. That event invades and reorders us; it alters the entire force field in which we live, making something new of us, not simply offering one among several alternative directions to us. And yet it talks to us, appears to us, finds us in familiar terms, ancient vocabularies, the old pictures and rhythms, however much transformed.

What makes gap-imagery so persuasive here is that we really do stretch across great openings between what we have received and what we are now experiencing to commit ourselves to all the god-images that inhabit us and all the traditions that inform us. We have no other way to develop a spiritual life, to find the healing strength of the imagination. As finite creatures in space and time we depend on these gap-filling images and grow our imaginative flesh around them.[6] They give us a hold on the divine. It matters immensely that we can in our imagination navigate across the gap and not fall in. For there madness threatens, and loss. Imaginative weavings across the great dark mysterious gap help prepare us for death, which must feel like being swallowed up in the gap. There is a handsome paradox in the fact that a religion can survive only by facing and dealing with death. The Judeo-Christian way is precise and rooted as it must be in the body, in time, in history: it is the way of resurrection in the flesh.

In the flesh? Yes, that is the whole point. We are created in the flesh; we are re-created in the flesh. That is the Christian faith, that is the figure of Jesus, God in the flesh. That is the scandalous fact at the center of everything for those who believe, the fact that the body in which we live our lives, the body in which we see others living their lives, the body in which we die to this life, is also the body of whatever it is that comes after this life. We call what comes *eternal life*, not eternal death. There can be no such thing as eternal death—even the weakest imagination can see that. If death is an end, a finality without reprieve, an absolute nothing, then *nothing* is the only word for it. Can one say *eternal nothing?* Perhaps, but all it can mean is nothing.

Everything we know we know in the flesh. Even the abstractions with which we must deal when we talk to each other have their meaning for us because they are connected to experiences we have had or can accept that others have had in the flesh. Do we speak of fulfillment, of emptiness, of drabness, of beauty, of truth, of goodness? Yes, of course we do, but we mean something precise when we say those fine round abstract words. We mean, whether we are prepared to admit it at the time or not, whether we can bring what we mean to fill consciousness in ourselves or not, something we have known in the flesh. We have in mind—or nerve, or gland, or spirit—a particular completion we have known, with an idea, with a belief, with a religious experience, a fulfillment we have felt in the flesh somewhere, somehow. And if we have any conviction at all when we speak of emptiness, it is because we have known its corroding vacancies in some form or another directly; we have known it in the flesh. So it is, too, with beauty and drabness and truth and goodness and all the rest. It is not simply a romantic notion that the great ennobling ideas or ideals by which all of us judge life to have fullness have their exact dwelling-places, a Grecian urn, say, or a Romanesque church. Nor is it just a poetic distemper to think of barrenness as the reduction of a great empire and its ruler to a heap of weathered stones and broken shards of glass in a desolate ancient landscape.[7] Our reality is a bodily reality; we have no other. The marvel is how much we can take in through our bodies, how far we can go in the flesh, without leaving the flesh. That is the power of what is housed in the flesh: the spirit, which is to say the person—that which makes each of us who and what we are, our own spirit, our own person, however much there may be of others in us as well.

It is because of the astonishing fact that each of us is himself or herself and nobody else, and that we know that to be a fact as we meet each other and come to know each other, in the flesh, that resurrection must be in the flesh. That doesn't mean we can be reduced to the flesh. We are very much more than the flesh. But what we are we know, and others know, because we reveal ourselves in the flesh. That is what must survive if anything survives, the miraculous amalgam of flesh and the spirit which is the human person. If we survive, we must do so in our fleshly specificity, with our particular thickness or thinness, our wisdom, our strength, our stupidity, our weakness, our love, our hope for love, our graces, our movings toward grace, our movings away. What we must find when we find ourselves forever is everything we have been, including what we tried to be, for even that incompleteness is ours; its failure to achieve being was part of our being.

When we look at our lives this way, contemplating death,

which is to say our death, that least abstract of things, we really find ourselves, yes even here below, find ourselves with some of the tinctures of what we will find when we find ourselves forever. What do we find? A name. A body. A life. A person who has lived a life with others, few or many, achieved much or not so much or little, but one who clearly has lived a life to which a name and a body and a term of days can be attached. A person thought worthy to be, or else there would be no such person.

Looking at life in the shadow of death—and all of us must at some time, in time, come to do that—is inevitably to face the possibility of life after death, of rebirth. This is for many, even believers, a stumbling block. Jesus, it may be, accomplished that, but he was God made man. Perhaps Lazarus and a few others whom Jesus touched can be allowed rebirth, but the rest of us? Come on! That strains the imagination. Does it? Pascal's musing on the subject is worth a moment's stretching of the imagination.

What "right," Pascal asks, do those who are unbelievers, atheists perhaps, "have to say that one cannot rise again?" Good scientist that he is, he asks the hard-nosed questions:

> Which is the more difficult, birth or resurrection; that what has never been should be, or that what has once been should recur? Is it more difficult to come into existence than to return to it? Habit makes the one seem easy for us, want of habit makes the other seem impossible; popular reasoning!

Pascal's scorn is unmistakable in the last two words. What a way to think, he is saying. He goes on, in the same meditative *Pensée,* to make a scornful comparison: "Why cannot a virgin bear a child? Does not a hen lay eggs without a cock? What distinguishes them outwardly from the others? And who has ever said that the hen cannot form the germ as well as the cock?" He is fixated on this subject. It is failure of the imagination that results in such conclusions about the articles of faith.

> What have they to say against the Resurrection and the Virgin Birth? Which is more difficult, to produce a man or an animal, or to reproduce one? And if they had never seen a certain species of animal, could they guess whether they were produced without collaboration?[8]

For Pascal, for all of us who live after the events of the gospels, and especially the resurrection, it is possible to be disdainful of those who will not believe, and worse still, those who will not ask themselves such questions as he does about birth and death. How cruel it is, with the example of Jesus and all who have believed in him and followed him, to have to go back into the same witlessness, the same fear and doubt, the same gaps in which so many of his immediate company were thrown after the crucifixion. Death can do that to us. Death will do that to us. It will bring everything we believe into question and reinforce all the ugly edges of our unbelief.

In the face of death all our imaginings about God seem to fall into the gap. In our time in history, how many have said that God is dead, God has disappeared, God is nowhere to be found. The stories of Jesus's death and resurrection tell us the same: his body was nowhere to be found. The visible outward manifestation of his presence, and the great high values he embodied, all gone with the missing corpse. But the story goes on to tell us that he rose again and appeared again, transformed, to the women who came to care for his body, and then appeared once more for his disciples. The great high values come again, embodied again, but in such changed form no one recognizes them at first, not even those who loved Jesus in the flesh.

In Matthew's telling of the story, Jesus's tomb is secured to guarantee that he who had died should stay dead. No renewal is to be claimed by his followers. But there is an earthquake, and a numinous being appears, and the guards at the tomb swoon in fright. It is they who become as dead men, telling us that if we seal ourselves up against renewal it will come anyway, but frighteningly, as a shaking of the earth we stand upon, of the very foundations of what supports us. If we want to guarantee that our God is dead and hold that, then we will become as dead guardians at the empty tomb, holding fast to our emptiness.[9]

But there are other ways. The women at the tomb are not sealed up against renewal. They receive the announcement from the numinous being, the angel at the tomb, that he who was dead has risen, they will see him, as will others at Galilee. So it is that we are opened to transformation of the flesh by the females among us, or symbolically, the feminine within us. This capacity which scripture identifies with the feminine can stand the "fear and joy" that the angel's announcement brings. The women at the tomb run to tell the others, acting as apostles to the apostles. And they hold to what they have seen, to what they know, even though they are not believed. This initial disbelief, from Jesus's closest followers, shows how hard it is to recognize old truths in new form, and with what distrust we receive the wisdom of the resurrected body. We are endlessly uneasy with those modes of being in us that are simply open to God.

The Magdalene, that great lover of Christ, receives the great news in Mark's gospel, and tells the others, and is not believed, but that does not make her disbelieve. In John's telling, Magdalene does not recognize Jesus until he calls her name. Though she cannot touch her teacher, she can see and accept that it is he, telling us that the new form of God's appearance brings with it an enabling power to see it and recognize it as connected to the old form and thus altogether receive it.

God comes to us across the gap, bringing us the capacity to let be what is before us, to look at it and take it in, and then respond to it. This showing of the new and transformed form that comes so unexpectedly brings with it an impetus, indeed a necessity, to tell others, to share it, to give it away. This we cannot receive without sharing. The women—all those Marys—stand in amazement and fear and joy, and then run to tell the others. This is not a private showing for a special group but a breaking into the lives of all of us, the receiving feminine in all of us receiving all of us into the world.

Jesus risen appears to two of the disciples in Mark, and again to a pair on the way to Emmaus. None of them recognizes him which can be taken to mean that a darkness of understanding, a thickness of feeling stand in the way of finding and recognizing the transformed, the resurrected. We need to be given special power and courage and determination to find it and see it and take it in. At Emmaus Jesus opens the disciples' eyes when he takes bread, breaks it and gives it to them. To Thomas who cannot even believe when Jesus stands there before him, Jesus goes even further, saying, Put your hand in my wound. Know me, he is saying, in the flesh. To all the disciples Jesus says, Touch me. I am a man, he is saying; a spirit does not have hands and feet.[10]

Jesus has been doing this always, appearing in the ordinary tasks of life. When John and Peter are fishing, Jesus tells them where to find their catch; he reveals himself when they break bread together. The literal taking in of food for the body opens the soul to its nourishment, to taking in transformed values, old truths made new. The life of the soul is always rooted in the body. The sacraments are always directed to enter the body.

When Jesus comes to his disciples as a new community made up of those who have seen his new form, the coming to them entails their going to others in the body. Jesus tells them, Go, teach, preach, feed, forgive, show visible signs of the invisible. God coming across the gap to us brings us the power to see and to receive and sends us on to others to share the transformation now taking up residence in our own bodies. That is what it means for Jesus to breathe on the disciples and say, Receive the Holy Spirit. The new value is personal and it is special for the soul and the body of humanity in the world. It enters history as well as the psyche; it changes individuals as well as society. We cannot have it for one without the other. To receive is to give. To give is to share. To share is to join in a new being that comes across the gap between our finite human images and God's infinite mystery to make us a new creation.

There are few stories in religious myth or tradition to match the challenge to the imagination of Jesus's descent into hell before rising up into heaven. We could take this as an allegory of the miraculous reforming of value which, as Jung says, will attain "supreme clarity of consciousness."[11] It also suggests a sinking far into the unconscious to establish a new order that goes, so to speak, all the way down into the places of unknowing in ourselves and in humanity. We are reordered from the bottom up.

When transformation of this kind breaks into our consciousness, so that we can recognize it and respond to its presence, it imposes upon us the ethical obligation to realize its values in daily life. We are claimed. This is what is entailed by the references to the mysterious new state that awaits us, not only at the end of time, but also in moments of seedling-like beginnings well before then.

Scripture speaks of a resurrected body, of a glorified body. These are akin to that mysterious state of which the alchemists wrote, that Jung called the subtle body.[12] The alchemists were on the whole good believing Christians and held to their faith while reaching toward this new state of the subtle body. What stands out in all these designations is the word "body." Body means an outward visible manifestation, something concrete, defined, a thing individually and distinctly expressive of personal life even though it appears in such an altered form that we can only grope our way toward it blindly and finally receive it as a gift, for we know we have no power to produce it ourselves, even though we expend every effort to be ready for its coming and pray every prayer to be able to receive it when it does.

The alchemists saw that the subtle body was partly physical and partly spiritual, a body that manifests itself in physical as well as mental forms. It exists, for them, in an intermediate realm between matter and psyche or soul, being neither one nor the other, but in some way both. In terms of depth psychology, the subtle body is like the transitional space in Winnicott's theory of the *me* and the *you* that originates in a baby's experiences of union with its mother just as it is separating from her and becoming conscious of mother-child relatedness.[13] The discovery and construction of this space of transition occurs in a young child's play with a favorite toy—the transitional object. The toy bear or lamb or monkey or piece of blanket really exists in the material world, but has an existence also as an imaginary being. The child imbues it with a personality, often with a name, and loves its characteristic smell and feel. What a child does then is both to find a favorite toy animal in the flesh and to create its being in the imagination. In the imaginative activity, the child finds its own self, which again it is also creating. Paradox marks this intermediate space, which like the subtle body is both found and created with the help of the imagination.

For the alchemists, imagination was the principal way of interaction with the matter they were trying to transform into spirit. Their famous attempt to wrest gold from a base metal, such as lead, was in fact a precious spiritualization of material things so that the body and indeed all of nature and the material world could be joined up with the redeeming action of Christ. In terms of depth psychology, we could say the alchemists both projected and found in matter the unconscious psyche. Their efforts to produce gold can be understood psychologically as an effort to achieve, not just a wholeness of personality, but a union of the whole person with the potential wholeness of creation, thus reinstating an Edenic paradise on earth.[14]

In modern clinical practice, the subtle body appears in the intermediate realm of projection between patient and analyst, where both are allowed to see the unconscious forces, complexes, and sub-personalities operating between them, bringing them together or interfering with their relationship. In such a seeing both persons are changed, both in a sense healed. It is imagination that brings about the healing. The wounding problems that bring a patient to analysis are visible in this imaginative seeing, as well as parallel wounds in the analyst.[15] Seeing these parts imaginatively and attempting to bring them together into a healing union is quite like the famous alchemical conjunction. The point for our meditations here on the resurrection is that an imaginative seeing shows us the unconscious in visible, concrete, and embodied ways. The unseen becomes seen and seems to gain as tangible a presence as ordinary material beings. Spirit takes on flesh.

Fleshification is what depth psychology is after. Its vision is of an unknowing unconscious place as something definitely there, as part of our reality and of all reality, missing nothing, not glowing surfaces at one extreme or the shabby undersides of society at the other.

All of us have the capacity for imaginative seeing. Imagination, as Jung discovered in his clinical work, is a piece of primordial being that we all possess.[16] Through it we achieve our firmest participation in being, reaching as far as the dual-nature of the God-man. In that hypostatic union of spirit and flesh, we know our citizenship in the world of country and nation, of jobs and taxes, of lovers and friends, of children and society. We live in the world of the imagination as fully, as spiritedly, as much with the organs of the body as we do in the blood and sinew activities of daily life. The special joy of the imagination is that with it we can reach to the source of both time and timelessness and find that support which will be the greatest of healing forces in our life.

We need to unite our egos with our imaginative selves, to put our time-centered parts in touch with the timeless source. We need to reach out to the conjunction of the alchemists. We are, in many ways, like hybrid creatures seeking unity. One part lives in a time-bound culture, works at a job, makes a home, votes. Another part of us reaches out to the sources of our being through primordial images that go all the way back in time and through time to the timeless. Our imagination comes into play when we face the unknown. For the alchemists it was in the workings of matter. For modern physics it is much the same when they face what Jung calls the "untrodden, untreadable regions." For depth psychology it happens when we recognize that there is more to us than what we are conscious of, that we too face "untrodden regions." Then, as Jung says, "the intermediate realm of subtle bodies comes to light again, and the physical and psychic are once more blended into indissoluble unity."[17] This is never more clear than when in our imagination we confront the unknown regions of death. Each of us knows the experience at some level of consciousness. When we allow ourselves full consciousness of it, the task falls on each of us to face the fact of death, to turn it over, and through it to construct connections to transcendent being as images of the timeless rise in us. At this conjunction of time and the timeless, we receive and participate in the life of the creator, however timidly and uncertainly. For we shape being now in the particular confines of our ego strengths and weaknesses, our physical personality and our psyche, our social group and language, our country and culture and epoch in history.

Because we are finite and particular every assertion we make now will appear both valid and invalid simultaneously. We cannot contain all that we touch imaginatively but must rely instead on its containing us, knowing and unknowing as our imagination knows and unknows, and often at the same time. Thus it matters a great deal how it happens and what happens when being comes to us across the gap, who and what comes to us and who and what takes us. What we receive comes to us in an embodied form, even though what we know from the meeting is clearly not all that could be known. Perhaps sometime—though it may be out of time—we will know.

What our imagination has brought us to, in this meeting of knowing and unknowing, is the eternal moment where our small being confronts Being itself. We are not stripped of our memory. We still possess our old god-images, the consolations that have come to us in prayer, all the sweetnesses and delights we have ever known. But they are our old clothes. We have put them aside. We have something new to wear now, something new to experience, something new to understand.

Existence is not enough now. Being is what we want. We are positively greedy for it. We want a wholeness that goes beyond the parts of things, that reaches beyond time, that holds everything together in the perfection of eternity. We are tired of things wearing out, bored with the task of replacing them, weary with all the naggings and fatuities of finitude. We want more than the thousand little deaths of the things that hasten into being, as St. Augustine puts it, only to show much more haste in making "not to be." Our flesh is slow, Augustine reminds us, because it is itself its own measure. That is good enough for ordinary fleshly purposes, as it is good enough, in the ways of the world, for an iron, a broom, a television set, even an automobile or a house to last just so long: "these things give way that other things may come in their places, and that the universe may be formed with all its parts." But Being is not a thing of parts and does not depart. Augustine's speaking Being asks, "As for me, do I ever go off to some other place?"

Choose Being, is Augustine's advice. That is where to build one's house, set one's trust, give over all one's uncertainties, one's dying appliances, one's decaying affections. There, all will be recovered, fadings refreshed, miseries healed. All will stay with us, with the God who remains with us always.[18] This is the wholeness our imagination longs for. This is the perfection we were born for. This is what we know and do not know, or rather what we do not dare to know, even when we are most filled with greed for being and our soul simply cries out to be enlarged, to grow bigger.

Augustine is the apostle of such growing in being, of such trusting in the faith which is the special truth of the resurrection of Jesus. Everything in holy writ counsels such trust and promises such growth for Augustine. See what he does with the last verses of the Latin version of Psalm 27—

> Wait for the Lord, do manfully;
> And let your heart be strengthened,
> And wait for the Lord.

In a splendid modern translation by Edmund Hill, we see how much Augustine makes of this waiting, and its promise of an eternal having and holding. It is where we find our true being, our all-encompassing sexuality, which is not, as a superficial reading of the passage may suggest, a diminishing of the female in a patriarchal asseveration of the male. Rather it is a repudiation of caricatures of gender and a gathering of all of us, male and female, into the manliness of the God-man. That is what he makes of the Latin text—*viriliter age,* "do manfully"—which he had before him, however much it may have altered the Hebrew, which says "take courage." "Let us listen now to the Lord's voice," he says, "the voice of him who is our father and our mother."

> He has noticed our grunts and groans, our puffing and blowing, he knows the one thing we are after, he has gladly received our petition for it at the hands of Christ, our good counsel. And until we finish our journey he says to us, 'Wait for the Lord, bear with him.' It isn't a cheat you will be waiting for, or a liar, or a bungler or someone who can't find anything to give you. It is the Almighty, the Faithful, the True, who has given you his word. So 'wait for the Lord, do manfully.' Don't give up, and become one of those it is said about 'Woe to those who lost endurance' [Ecclesiasticus 2:16]. Wait for the Lord. It is said to all of us, and it is said to one man, because we are all one man in Christ, all of us who are longing for one thing, and who trust in these days of our evils that we shall see the good things of the Lord in the land of the living. 'Do manfully, and let your heart be strengthened, and wait for the Lord.' The man who fails to wait and endure has become effeminate, he has lost his manhood. This is advice though for women as well as men, because all of us are one man in Christ, in whom there is neither male nor female [Galatians 3:28]. Let your heart be strengthened and wait for the Lord. By waiting for him you will possess him, to have and to hold for ever. Unless of course you can find anything greater, anything better, anything sweeter to desire; in that case by all means set your heart on that.[19]

What is happening is that we are being faced with a God who comes right up to us and then disappears, as if irretrievably lost, and then comes again, speaking now of the resurrected body, of the glorified body. The highest value, which we thought was dead, will rise up. It will not be concealed from us but will appear with such splendor and brilliance that it will rivet us to its glory. The particular way we define our nature, in the body, will continue to be our way, but transformed into a new state, a state that promises to come to all of us and to bring all of us to it. Individuality exists, after all, not in spiritual abstraction, in the conjunction of all our parts, not in separation, but as we are brought together, joined mystically in the body of Christ.

The resurrected body is promised to us after death. It is that promised body our imagination brings before us as we face the unknown terrain of death. Jung, like Augustine and the fathers, advises us to entertain and meditate upon images for death and the life beyond.[20] This will protect us from the regressive pull of images from our past which many of us succumb to as we grow old. Over and over, we repeat stories of school or early home life or ancient jobs of work. We dwell in the past and lose contact with our children, with our friends, with our own selves in the present. We do not meet the challenge of the unknown of our present life. Here is where we must join our own images of death and the afterlife with the images our religious traditions present to us of the resurrected body and let our imaginations play across the gap between them. None of these images of death and the next world, wherever they came from, can really reach across the gap of death to the other side, the great unknown, but they can ready us for what comes. In this way, imagination helps us correspond with grace.[21]

Resurrection points to a life after death, but we are given glimpses of it here, now, in this life. How? We meet it in our prayer life. We can even come upon it in our social and political life. It is a matter of imagination. Our pictures for God precede any speaking about God as inevitably they do any speaking to God, for our images touch us all the way down in our bodies, arousing reactions of pulse and breath, of posture and gesture. Our images stir our emotions as well as our thoughts, our spiritual longings as well as our dread. Images from this realm arrive unbidden, startling us, and arrive sometimes long after all our arduous efforts to create them seem to have failed. Often we do not understand them; rarely do we forget them. They come in dreams, sometimes like an official announcement from an authoritative source, more often as a numinous image. A woman dreamt a "dream statement" which revealed to her a deep meaning of one of the beatitudes that had always escaped her:

"You do not get a backlog of love. You must always spend it. Hence you will always be poor and will always see God." That is one good if rare sort of visitation. More often, god-images in dreams come as puzzling pictures, such as the dream of another woman that made her feel linked to a good self within her from which she could live, which she could believe in and trust. The dream felt all the more important to her because she usually felt herself to be absent from things or only a jumble of fragmented impulses. She dreamt she was swimming in the ocean; "a joyous porpoise-like creature came and swam alongside me, diving and jumping, swooping with joy, wanting me to join in."

Our social groups can supply us with god-images. The longing for a God who sits with us in our actual situations, both good and bad, issues in god-images of color, as in black theology, or of a particular sex, as in feminist theology, or a particular political posture, such as the god of the oppressed in liberation theology. God-images participate in our actual being and become a god of the whole or true or bigger self within our psyches, as in Jung's archetype of the Self. These group-gods express a differentiation of the traditional god-image that for many has come to feel too abstract or distant. When traditional symbols for God degenerate into signs, the abstract god-image may appear, say, as white and male, crying out to some for images of different color, sex, and politics. Competition among people's god-images sadly bespeaks a symbolic poverty where we mistake images for the real thing and our symbols regress to symbolic equations. We need to remember that all these are merely our pictures for God, human, finite, fallible, never complete, never to be equated with God.[22]

Our faith itself and its many lines of tradition offer us beguilingly different images for God. The biblical imagination ranges as far as a God pictured in inanimate terms—as rock, citadel, thick darkness, unending light. God comes with great wings under which we can shelter ourselves, as a fashion designer creating the ephod in Exodus, as architect of the temple, as hovering presence over the mercy seat above the ark in the Holy of Holies. God appears as a dinner-party host, as wonderful counselor, as still small voice, as one who baptizes in fire. The great mystics give us still more pictures to prod our imagination —of the innermost room in our Interior Castle (Teresa of Avila), as "fruitive darkness" and "sparkling stone" (Ruysbroeck), as a great all-seeing eye looking back at us (Jacob Boehme).[23]

In our prayer lives we need to place our personal and group god-images, gathered from the present, beside all these gathered from the past and let our imagination weave connections among them. In that way tradition feeds us and we feed tradition. Imaginative prayerful meditation always brings us more connection to self and to others, to our psyches as well as to our spirits.

We must remember that our personal images for God arise in large part from our own projections and introjections, from what we take in from the world around us and put out into it. Thus to identify our pictures of God must bring consciousness of left-out pieces of our selves. A man dreaming of Jesus cursing because of the agony of the cross comes up against his denial of his own suffering, which clamors to be seen, responded to, and expressed by him.[24]

Our god-images rise up between parts of ourselves and in our relationship with others, forcing into consciousness the great currents of our lives. Our god-images make palpable the possibilities that operate in the realm of the subtle body, in the spaces that live inside us individually and between and among us in groups. Hermann Broch had the genius to give life to this realm in his novels as did Robert Musil. We are made conscious of a collective spiritual longing for salvation in Broch's *Death of Virgil*, of a collective madness waiting to break out into the psychopathology of the Nazis as in Musil's *Man Without Qualities.*[25] Works of art and religion sometimes force into our consciousness the invisible but very influential subtle-body factors operating in the transitional space among us. We are put on notice: no more denial.

In the struggles of our prayer life, sometimes lasting many years, sooner or later we must come to the end of all images— our own, our group's, those of our tradition. We reach the far end of the shores of our known country. Having identified the images that operate in us and among us, having gained more self, more life together as a result, greater access to tradition, suddenly we come to a stop. It is almost as if time has come to a stop. We disidentify from our images. We have reached the end of the ladder of images that has for so long supported and eased our praying. We peer into the gap, beyond all ends, and see no way to cross. What we relied upon no longer works. We cannot get to God from our side. With all our heightened consciousness, our development, our great struggles and enlightened responses, our new knowledge, still we do not reach God. The God who has created us as image-makers now breaks our images, smashes all our images for the divine. They do not create God for us any more or in any way secure God in relation to us. Relation to God is God's gift alone to give, along with the accompanying grace to receive it.

As in the dark night of John of the Cross, what happens now results from God working on the soul, not from the soul's own efforts. Our finite images have reached their end. We are forced to let go of them, which is terribly painful and makes us feel that something precious has died. This is death in life. We suffer feelings of irretrievable loss. The sacrament or theological symbol that connected us to God lies broken, powerless.[26] Our methods of praying, once so effective in bringing us into God's presence, are useless to us. The relation to spouse or child that carried the divine connection into our daily life may be disrupted, whether by death or infidelity or rebellion. What we have relied upon in the past to anchor us in God has been cut loose. We do not know where we are. We wander in the dark. A radical disidentification may come upon us, summoned by a force that breaks all the rules. Now a different kind of love beckons. A decisive break with our work, with all that has seemed permanent in our lives, may command us to pursue a new path, to leave all authority as we have understood it in rule and procedure. We are cast out, pushed toward the unknown.

Such disidentification happens in social and political life, too, where all our fervor and action to implement our highest values, to effect justice, to bring peace, to preserve the planet, may hit impasse.[27] Our participation in specific social actions that seemed to mediate our participation in God now feels meaningless. We cannot go on with them. We feel disillusioned with the political process; our position papers, our marches, seem empty. We wander in the darkness.

But which darkness is it? Is it the darkness of deficiency and disaffection, which is not true darkness at all but simply an absence of light? Or is it the darkness of the dark night of the soul, the tutoring darkness which reveals the light. The false darkness is the bleakness we face when the world is too much with us, when we are too intent on getting somewhere, on making *our* justice prevail, *our* truth, *our* map of being. This is the meaninglessness that T.S. Eliot compares to the riders in the London underground:

> Only a flicker
> Over the strained time-ridden faces
> Distracted from distraction by distraction
> Filled with fancies and empty of meaning

"Not here," he concludes, "Not here the darkness in this twittering world."[28]

The true darkness is the *Noche oscura* of St. John of the Cross, the dark night that is "fired with love's yearnings," where we are without the consolations and delights of worldly things but also dispossessed of the obstacles to the union with Being that their beguiling shapes and forms may provide. We have not yet the guidance of an enlightened understanding nor the satisfaction of arrival at our destination.[29] We are at an impasse. We live in ambiguity, but it is a blessed ambiguity, for it is one we share with Jesus, who must always be ambiguous to our clouded understanding, for he was with us and left us and yet is still with us. "But," says Dietrich Bonhoeffer, who never tired of stressing the ambiguity of the Christ figure,

> the truth is that if this earth was good enough for the Man Jesus Christ, if a man like him really lived in it, then, and only then, has life a meaning for us. If Jesus had not lived, then our life, in spite of all the other people we know and honour and love, would be with-

> out meaning. No doubt we often forget in such times as these the meaning and purpose of our profession. But is this not the simplest way of putting it? The word "meaning" does occur in the Bible, but it is only a translation of what the Bible means by "promise."[30]

At moments of impasse, whether in psyche or soul, in prayer or social action, we do not believe that if we surrender to the darkness that engulfs us new visions, solutions, or energies will suddenly burst upon us. We feel helpless to fix things, resourceless. And yet in this dying, in this death, there is a suddenness, the suddenness of absolute beginnings: the resurrected one comes across the gap to meet us. He brings a whole new picture that we could not reach by ourselves. It breaks in upon us, this new picture, like him who brought it. It creates new life.

Such a breaking-in can happen in our prayer and imaginative life. Or it can happen socially, where a new possibility, completely different from what we have expected, shows itself in political and social worlds. The early work of Martin Luther King, Jr., meeting violence with nonviolence, meeting racist division with a vision of love, reaching both oppressors and oppressed, showed us such a breaking-in. It happens psychologically too, when a new image of sexuality, spirituality, or aggression leaps up in us, suddenly throws us to the ground, causing total reversion from what we were before, a new conversion. Jungian psychology offers vivid illustration of this experience both in theory and in practice. It comes in the exercises of Jung's method of active imagination, where we open our attention to whatever the psyche shows us and engage in imaginative dialogue with an autonomous other.[31] To see this other as other, our ego must remain firmly settled in its own ground and commitments, and know that there is no preordained outcome to the imaginative encounter. That is what makes the method so scary, so dangerous.

The autonomy of the unconscious shocks us, may even pull us under, so that we lose our foothold in reality. Then no dialogue is possible. And even if we escape that danger, we must recognize that the way the other side "speaks" will be very different from speech as we usually meet it, within ourselves or with others. It may communicate through frightening images or seductive ones. It may communicate through our body, making us feel exhilarated or full of aches and pains. It may shout back at us through noisy symptoms or may entirely elude us, looking to fold its skirts and disappear into the desert. The unconscious has its own logic which is not always the same as our conscious one. That is what we learn when we dare a full prayer life. Sooner or later come struggle and fear. We know that the Spirit really exists and God really has come into our world. Something must happen. But what? And will we be up to it? These are the fearful questions we ask when we seek God's presence, with no holds barred.

We know what happens to begin with—our god-images are broken. What do we do then? Consider this example. A woman used her imagination to put herself in the position of the woman in the gospels who had hemorrhaged for twelve years and dared, in her misery, to touch Jesus as part of a great crowd and was healed. The modern woman went back in her imagination to a hot dusty village square where many people were gathered around Jesus. She dragged herself forward to touch him. Now her imagination took its own autonomous turn; it was too crowded for her. She gave up, lay in the dust. Jesus, leaving, from some fifty feet away turned to her and said, "What do you want?" She fumbled for words, stammered, said to him, "I suffer; I am divided, and pulled apart." Jesus looked at her directly and said, "That is your cross and you will have to bear it." "Bear it!" she screamed in anger. "You talk! Just you wait! You are going to be crucified and many will be killed in your name!" With that, she drew an axe out of an Indian leather shoulder-holster and threw it at Jesus, fully intending to hit him. Jesus reached up effortlessly and caught the axe lightly in his hand, then turned and walked away.[32] Her imagination not only brought home to the woman her need to claim her own aggression but absolutely broke her image of Jesus as tender and mild. An entirely other Jesus confronted her to match and encourage the differences in herself.

Some years later, after much digestion of the axe-throwing

incident, the woman again imagined she was the gospel woman who had hemorrhaged for so many years: "I waited for Jesus to come . . . this time alone. 'Lord,' I said, 'I cannot bear this suffering any longer. You must help me to bear this cross.' Again Jesus turned to walk away from me. I grabbed Jesus around the knees and refused to let go. But Jesus did not in fact struggle to get away. He stood his ground. Slowly, however, he sank to his knees and lay down by me, with my head resting against his legs. For three or four days I held this image in my mind. In it, I never once released my grip. Slowly, on the fourth day of my imaginings, Jesus reached down and caressed my hair. My aching arms let go. He rose, drawing me to my feet. As he held me near him, blood came pouring out of his mouth, covering me, bathing me from head to toe. Then the blood poured into my mouth and I thought, 'Surely I will choke.' Months later, thinking about this image, I began to hum an old half-forgotten hymn:

> There is a fountain filled with blood,
> Drawn from Emmanuel's veins.
> And sinners plunged beneath that flood
> Lose all their guilty stains."

We see here the way the numinous can break in, boldly crossing the gap between us and the divine. Now again we must ask, What then happens to us? The answer is, we think, that we are liberated from the literal. We deconstruct our accustomed ways of seeing. Little epiphanies break in upon us, in which we lose the mediated presence of God only to find the immediate experience of God coming right to us, into our inner seeing and outer living. Our theology shifts. We move from depending on God to protect us, with a full set of images to support us, to learning how to protect God from our god-images.[33] Our questions shift, no longer to ask who we are, but rather who this is coming through to us.

Psychologically, the question now is how we are to house this great subject who takes up residence in us, who de-centers us, who radically rearranges the core from which we live. Theologically, we ask what it means to live with this tremendous stranger so near. The dualities of subject and object soften and almost disappear. We live in an other and that other lives in us.[34] A joyousness pervades our life; we enjoy a simple happiness in being. From it springs a whole new set of acts and attitudes with, toward, and from others. There is now a motivation for good in us drastically different from doing good works out of fear or guilt or urge to power. Evil appears as that force of deficiency, that absence, that acts to blight a simple happiness in being. It pierces us as it pierced Jesus, whose blood as a result flowed into the world. Now our blood joins this flow, and our love moves with it, in acts large and small. This is living for, in, and by the glory of God. God is no longer an object of contemplation, an idea to be thought, but a presence, a continuing one. The medium of relation to God no longer can be thought of as concept, symbol, ritual, or cause. It is instead a mingling of presences in our soul.[35]

We live in paradoxes, impasses, and ambiguities; that is what we have learned. We get beyond the gap only if we are firmly rooted on our side, in the flesh, in communities of believers, in what we believe. This body, so concrete, so finite, is what decays, but this body is also what is raised. This, finally, is what happens. It happens at the end of time, yet we experience it ahead of time, in little bits and pieces of time. Then God comes down to us in the flesh, for a fleeting moment—and changes everything. Conflict still exists but it is transfigured, held within a great unity. We still see and experience the ordinary things, people, events, but they too are transfigured. Knowing joins the unknowing that lives in us as the unconscious. Our personal illumination feeds out of and into a shared vision of life with others. God, crossing the gap, ends all the stopping-places of religion, destroying the mediating structures with immediate experience. Each subjective religious language tries to establish itself as objective truth and each is then brought to an end. It is our never-ending task to distinguish between faith in the wholly other who draws so near to us even as it directs us out of time and belief in a religious object that in time seems more and more distant.[36]

What brings the religious object close—and closer than

close, right within us—is when it breaks all the boundaries of time and space to share our subjectivity with us. That is the astonishing truth of the faith and its psychological and spiritual strength. We live as one in the human and the divine, each of us, because the divine became human. When St. Paul says, "For him, who knew no sin, he was made sin for us, that we might be made the righteousness of God in him," he is not speaking in metaphors. He is describing a transformation of the very root of the human. The Greek word which is variously translated as righteousness, justice, holiness, the good—*dikaiosunei*—means, in effect, that when Jesus Christ became man, and took on all the vulnerabilities of the human, we became capable of doing all that was right and good and true. For Jesus, the possibility of sin; for us, the choice to be holy.[37]

The psychological reach of this central fact of the faith is stunning. It is what resolves impasse and dissolves ambiguity. It is resurrection in the flesh, here and now, as well as in the eternal distance. We possess the life that was laid down for us. We have been crucified with Christ, as Paul says of himself in the grand statement explaining himself to the Galatians, and yet we live in the flesh, now. "I live now, not I, but Christ in me," are the famous words that say so much, that insist that we have been resurrected, that the violence of the crucifixion has been matched, and overmatched, by the violence done to our habitual ways of thinking and feeling and understanding. We who live now, not we, but Christ in us, have been reborn.[38]

But is it true? Did it really happen, then, in Jerusalem, that believable unbelievable, impossible actual event, the resurrection? And does it really still happen to us who live in a world bemused by grotesque rituals of the posthumous, celebrating the post-modern and the post-Christian, erecting monuments to the trivialization of the human and the divine?

The answer does not come to us in the ordinary way of knowledge. As the resurrection requires a rearrangement of our understanding of what it means to live and to die, of being itself, so does it command a transformation of our ways of knowing. In this experience of rebirth our subjectivity has been invaded; we share it now—we speak in such strange words as "Not I, but

Christ in me." And so, too, has the object been transformed, for what we know is what we are. And we are not less ourselves because of the change, but more. We have gained being. All that we have been so greedy for has been added, and added a thousandfold. Our souls have been enlarged; they really are bigger. It is not now so much that we know these things, but that we and these things are known where knowing and being are the same. It is a task to grasp all of this, but we have the resources.

Imagination accomplishes the task again and again and again. Imagination is the necessary structure of thought, the only possible one, about the unconditioned wholly other which is the Holy. In imagination, we can see the subtle body. In imagination, we can reach objectivity and live our daily round with joy, drawing from the reservoir of being enthusiasm for being. How? We let the images be there, let them come to us. We see them; we look into them. We reflect on them. We respond to them in them. That is the healing imagination.

Notes

Chapter 1: The Healing Imagination

1. See Ann Belford Ulanov, "The Christian Fear of the Psyche," in *Picturing God* (Cambridge: Cowley, 1986).

2. C.G. Jung, *Letters*, eds. G. Adler, A. Jaffé, trans. R.F.C. Hull (Princeton: Princeton University Press, 1973), vol. I., p. 60.

3. All examples of psychological material from psychotherapy, unless otherwise noted, are from the psychoanalytical practice of Ann Ulanov, with gratitude to those persons involved for their permission to use them.

It is not uncommon to find a suicidal person's recovery to life manifested in a project of redecorating a house, or clearing land, or other such reconstructive activities. This can be a way of slowly rebuilding the psyche.

4. Mandelstam's point was that poetry was frightening enough to Russia's despotic rulers to kill poets for the sentiments expressed in their verses. See the introduction to Irina Ratushinskaya's poems *Beyond the Limit*, by one of her translators, Frances Padorn Brent (Evanston: Northwestern University Press, 1987), p. xii. Ratushinskaya underlined the significance of this fact about herself and Mandelstam in a talk at Barnard College on February 23, 1988.

5. For example, see Elizabeth Petroff, *Consolation of the Blessed* (New York: Alta Gaia Society, 1959), pp. 63–65, 68, 71.

6. See Samuel Coleridge, *Biographia Literaria* (London: Bell, 1894), p. 41.

7. For a discussion of how we make heaven and hell for each other, see Ann Belford Ulanov, "Heaven and Hell" in *Picturing God.*

8. See "The Toad," in Gertrud Kolmar, *Dark Soliloquy,* trans. H.A. Smith (New York: Seabury, 1975), p. 133. The second stanza is sharply illustrative:

I am the toad.
I love the stars of night,
The coals of sunset, evening's ruddy lode,
Smoulder in purple ponds, barely alight.
Beneath the rain barrel's sodden wood
I crouch, low, fat, and wise.
My painful moon-eyes wait and brood
To view the sun's demise.

9. Karl Menninger, *The Vital Balance* (New York: Viking, 1963), chap. XVI.

10. See Gaston Bachelard, *The Poetics of Reverie,* trans. Daniel Russell (New York: Orion Press, 1969), p. 1.

11. See John Wren-Lewis, "Love's Coming of Age," in Charles Rycroft, ed., *Psychoanalysis Observed* (New York: Coward-McCann, 1966), p. 106: ". . . the root of human alienation lies not in economics or politics but in personal life itself, at the most intimate level where each person faces (or avoids facing) his own inner life, and is involved in relationships with other individuals on the basis of recognizing them (or directly refusing to recognize them) as beings with the same kind of inner life." See also Rycroft's *Imagination and Reality* (New York: International Universities Press, 1968); and Garrett Green, *Imaging God: Theology and the Religious Imagination* (San Francisco: Harper & Row, 1989).

12. See *Biographia Literaria,* p. 144.

13. See "Freud and Jung: Contrasts," in C.G. Jung, *Collected Works,* vol. 4, trans. R.F.C. Hull (New York: Pantheon, 1961), pp. 339–340 (pars. 783–784).

14. See Otto Rank, *Psychology and The Soul,* trans. W.D. Turner (New York, Perpetua, 1961), pp. 37, 176, 191–192.

15. Such images rush upon us in prayer. See Ann and Barry

Ulanov, *Primary Speech: A Psychology of Prayer* (Philadelphia: John Knox-Westminster, 1982), chaps. 4 and 5.

16. Jung developed a method called "active imagination," to engage imaginative contents and receive what "they" had to communicate. See C.G. Jung, *Mysterium Coniunctionis,* trans. R.F.C. Hull (New York: Pantheon, 1983), *CW* 14, pp. 495–496 (par. 706). See also Barbara Hannah, *Encounters with the Soul: Active Imagination* (Santa Monica: Sigo Press, 1981); see also Janet Dallett, "Active Imagination in Practice," in *Jungian Analysis,* ed. Murray Stein (La Salle: Open Court, 1982); see also Michael Fordham, "The Self as Imaginative Construct," *Journal of Analytical Psychology,* 24, 1, 1979.

17. See Sigmund Freud, "Formulations on the Two Principles of Mental Functioning," *Standard Edition,* vol. 12, trans. James Strachey (London: Hogarth Press, 1958). See also C.G. Jung, "Two Kinds of Thinking," in *Symbols of Transformation, CW* 5, trans. R.F.C. Hull (Princeton: Princeton University Press, 1956).

18. Many artists have made this point, none more stubbornly than Henry Moore. See Geoffrey Shaterley and Stephen Spender, *Henry Moore: Sculptures in Landscape* (New York: Clarkson Potter/Crown, n.d.), pp. 30, 34.

19. For a discussion of the seminal importance of play, see D.W. Winnicott, *Playing and Reality* (New York: Basic Books, 1971), chapters 3 and 4. See also, Erik H. Erikson, *Toys and Reasons* (New York: Norton, 1977); Erik H. Erikson, "Play and Actuality," Lois Barclay Murphy, "Infant's Play and Cognitive Development" in *Play and Development,* ed. Maria W. Piers (New York: Norton, 1972); Paul W. Pruyser, *The Play of the Imagination* (New York: International Universities Press, 1983); D. Davidson, "Playing and the Growth of Imagination," *The Journal of Analytical Psychology,* 24, 1, 1979.

20. Ann Belford Ulanov, *The Wisdom of the Psyche* (Cambridge: Cowley, 1988), p. 48.

21. Jung's famous house dream is reported in his autobiography, *Memories, Dreams, Reflections,* ed. Aniela Jaffé, trans. Richard and Clara Winston (New York: Pantheon, 1963), pp.

158–159. Bachelard discusses it in *The Poetics of Space*, trans. Maria Jolas (New York: Orion Press, 1964), p. xxxiii.

22. See D.W. Winnicott, *Human Nature* (London: Free Association Books, 1988), pp. 42, 67–68, 84, 118, 122.

23. See by His Holiness Tenzin Gyatso The Fourteenth Dalai Lama, "The Practices of the Bodhisattvas," trans. Jeffrey Hopkins, in *The Christ and the Bodhisattva*, ed. Donald S. Lopez, Jr. and Steven C. Rockefeller (Albany: SUNY Press, 1987), p. 217.

24. See C.G. Jung, *Psychology and Alchemy*, trans. R.F.C. Hull (New York: Parthenon, 1953), *CW* 12, p. 220 (par. 334).

25. It is a fearful task, as Eliot says many times in the *Quartets*, an "intolerable wrestle With words and meanings," in which there is always the difficult fact, for Eliot, that "There is. . . . At best, only a limited value In the Knowledge derived from experience." See *Four Quartets*, in *The Complete Poems and Plays* (New York: Harcourt Brace, 1952), p. 125.

26. For a discussion of corresponding with grace, see Ann and Barry Ulanov, *Cinderella and Her Sisters: The Envied and the Envying* (Philadelphia: Westminster, 1983), chap. 13.

Chapter 2: The Gap

1. For a discussion of this dream, see Ann Belford Ulanov, "The Self as Other," in *Carl Jung and Christian Spirituality*, ed. Robert L. Moore (Mahwah: Paulist Press, 1988).

2. Winnicott says our fear of falling forever is one of the ways we have known a split-second of madness since infancy. See D.W. Winnicott, "Ego Integration in Child Development," in his *The Maturational Processes and the Facilitating Environment* (New York: International Universities Press, 1965), pp. 57–58. See also, D.W. Winnicott, "Fear of Breakdown," in his *Psychoanalytic Explorations*, eds. Clare Winnicott, Ray Shepherd, Madeleine Davis (London: Karnac Books, 1989).

3. See Lola Paulsen, "Dreams and Fantasy of Falling," *Journal of Analytic Psychology*, 16, 1, 1971.

4. See "God's Grandeur," "Duns Scotus's Oxford," and

"Henry Purcell," in *The Poems of Gerard Manley Hopkins,* ed. W.H. Gardiner and N.H. MacKenzie (London: Oxford University Press, 1967), pp. 66, 79, 80; and *The Letters of Gerard Manley Hopkins to Robert Bridges,* ed. C.C. Abbott (London: Oxford University Press, 1935), pp. 168–169.

5. Cited in Marion Milner, *On Not Being Able to Paint* (New York: International Universities Press, 1979), p. 25, from J. Gasquet, *Cézanne.*

6. See St. Gregory the Great, *Morals on the Book of Job,* VI:18 (London: Walter Smith, 1883), I, 324–325.

7. C.G. Jung "Archetypes of the Collective Unconscious" in *The Archetypes and the Collective Unconscious,* trans. R.F.C. Hull, *CW* 9:1 (New York: Pantheon, 1959), p. 8 (par. 11). Re Jung and animals, see also Jung, *Alchemical Studies,* trans. R.F.C. Hull (Princeton: Princeton University Press, 1967) *CW* 13, pp. 282–283, (pars. 364–365); see also Jung, *Mysterium Coniunctionis, CW* 14, p. 214 (par. 283) and *Symbols of Transformation, CW* 5, pp. 269, 271 (pars. 264, 411, 415).

8. See Marion Milner, "The Framed Gap" in *The Suppressed Madness of Sane Men* (London: Tavistock, 1987), pp. 80–81.

9. The succinct Latin formula is a reduction of Romans 1:20.

10. Blake's is not the only translation of the Trinity into such compressed terms; it is all but a commonplace of medieval iconography.

11. "The soul, when it is involved with what is mortal and fragile, maintains its authority with great difficulty and intently straining," says St. Augustine in his *De Musica.* See the translation by W.F. Jackson Knight, *St. Augustine's De Musica: A Synopsis* (London: Orthological Institute, n.d.), p. 94.

12. Gapless films are unthinkable. It would take hours just to move from one end of a set to another; it would make the brilliant indirection of the great directors impossible; films without gaps would, as it were, be faithless.

13. See "The Location of Cultural Experience" in Winnicott, *Playing and Reality,* p. 117.

14. See A.B. Ulanov, "Picturing God," in *Picturing God.*

15. See A. and B. Ulanov, *Primary Speech: A Psychology of Prayer*, chap. 4.

16. Winnicott, *Human Nature*, p. 60; see also Melanie Klein, "The Importance of Symbol-Formation in the Development of the Ego," in *Love, Guilt and Reparation & Other Works 1921–1945* (New York: Delacorte Press/Seymour Lawrence, 1975).

17. Winnicott expresses his relief and excitement in reading Darwin's *Origin of the Species*. He saw ". . . that gaps in knowledge need not scare me. For me this idea meant a great lessening of tension and consequently a release of energy for work and play." Cited in Adam Phillips, *Winnicott* (London: Fontana, 1988), p. 1.

18. Petroff, *Consolation of the Blessed*, pp. 75ff.

19. "Self-object" is a term coined by the psychoanalyst Heinz Kohut who developed the school of Self Psychology. It means any object (primarily a person, but also a house, a dog, a god, or any other who becomes an object of our attention) which we relate to by referring it to ourselves, to mirror our feelings, thoughts, and needs, indeed our whole being. In contrast, an objective object is one we recognize as existing in its own right. We have need of both kinds of objects our whole life. See Heinz Kohut, "Self-Self Object Relationships Reconsidered," in his *How Does Analysis Cure?* ed. Arnold Goldberg and Paul Stepansky (Chicago: University of Chicago Press, 1984).

20. Knitting is a central sign in the theology of Lady Julian of Norwich. We are knit together with God. See Julian of Norwich, *The Revelations of Divine Love*, trans. James Walsh, S.J. (London: Burns and Oates, 1961), chap. 57.

21. Winnicott, *Human Nature*, p. 127.

22. See T.S. Eliot, *The Family Reunion*, II; i, in *The Complete Poems and Plays* (New York: Harcourt, Brace, 1952), pp. 270–271.

23. For a discussion of twoness and oneness see Michael Eigen, "Dual Union or Undifferentiation? A Critique of Marion Milner's View of The Sense of Psychic Creativeness," *International Review of Psycho-Analysis*, (1983) 10, 415. See also, Marion Milner, *The Suppressed Madness of Sane Men*, pp. 289–292.

24. Milner writes: ". . . can we summarize what the will has

to do? It seemed that it certainly has to wait in very active present mindedness and be content with being a frame, holding the empty space if something new is to emerge. . . . can we say that it has to recognize its limited function, give up any hoped for omnipotence, and bow before the more powerful imagination? 'Oh human imagination, oh divine body I have thee crucified,' wrote William Blake. 'As dying yet behold we live,' says St. Paul. I told too how often experiencing the pattern-making aspect of the imagination begins to feel like an answering presence, even a 'you.' . . . I had even come to look on many of the sayings in the Gospels as providing a handbook for the process of creative activity." See "1952: The Framed Gap," in *The Suppressed Madness of Sane Men*, p. 82.

25. See Paul Ricoeur, *Freud and Philosophy: An Essay on Interpretation*, trans. Dennis Savage (New Haven: Yale University Press, 1970), pp. 530–531.

26. Too often the election of Job to special intercessor for his scornful friends is glossed over. See Job 42:8. For a discussion of this crucial passage, see Barry Ulanov, "Job and His Comforters," in *The Bridge*, ed. J.M. Oesterreicher (New York: Pantheon, 1958), pp. 264–266.

27. See John Macquarrie, *Martin Heidegger* (Richmond: John Knox, 1968), p. 50.

Chapter 3: Madness

1. See, for example J.N. Grou, *Manual for Interior Souls* (London: Burns & Oates & Washbourne, 1952); see also Maurice Nédoncelle, *The Nature and Use of Prayer*, trans. A. Manson (London: Burns & Oates, 1962), p. 89.

2. See St. John of the Cross, *Ascent of Mount Carmel*, chap. 23 where he says "the soul must needs withdraw from all apprehensible kinds of knowledge," in *The Complete Works*, trans. E.A. Peers (Westminster: Newman Press, 1964), vol. 1, p. 214, in contradistinction to his own performance, dealt with at some length in Barry Ulanov, "The Song of Songs: The Rhetoric of

Love," in *The Bridge,* ed. J.M. Oesterreicher, Vol. IV (New York: Pantheon, 1962), pp. 89–118.

3. See, for a discussion of the complexities of sexual identity by the same writer, White's mixture of autobiography, literary theory, and the place of the literary imagination in modern society, *Flaws in the Glass: A Self-Portrait* (London: Jonathan Cape, 1981).

4. For a discussion of these two types of thinking, see Ann and Barry Ulanov, *Religion and the Unconscious* (Philadelphia: Westminster, 1975), chap. 1.

5. See Winnicott, *Human Nature,* pp. 43–48; see also D.W. Winnicott, "This Feminism," in his *Home Is Where We Start From,* ed. Clare Winnicott, Ray Shepherd, Madeline Davis (New York: Norton, 1986); see also A.B. Ulanov, *Receiving Woman,* chap. 3.

6. For discussions of this inevitable process of introjection and projection, see Marie-Louise von Franz, *Projection and Re-Collection in Jungian Psychology,* trans. William H. Kennedy (La Salle: Open Court, 1980), chaps. 1–3. See also Melanie Klein, "Our Adult World and Its Roots in Infancy," in her *Envy and Gratitude & Other Works 1946–1963* (New York: Delacorte, 1975), and Ann and Barry Ulanov, *The Witch and the Clown: Two Archetypes of Human Sexuality* (Wilmette: Chiron, 1987), chaps. II and IX, for examples of how these timeless figures turn up in individual persons' experiences.

7. For a discussion of fatness as a means of entry to a larger central self, see A.B. Ulanov, "Fatness and the Female," *Psychological Perspectives,* vol. 10, Fall 1979. For images of the mother deity, see Erich Neumann, *The Great Mother: An Analysis of the Archetype,* trans. Ralph Manheim (Princeton: Princeton University Press, 1970).

8. For a discussion of this primary mode of experiencing, see A. and B. Ulanov, *Religion and the Unconscious,* chap. 1.

9. For a discussion of imaginative elaboration of body functioning, see Winnicott, *Human Nature,* pp. 51–52.

10. For a discussion of the scapegoat complex, see Ann Belford Ulanov, "The Double Cross," in *Lingering Shadows: Jung*

and Anti-Semitism, ed. A. Maidenbaum (Boulder: Shambala, 1990).

11. The witch drains the life-blood out of our conscious living into repetitive obsessive fantasies and parody symbolization. See A. and B. Ulanov, *The Witch and the Clown,* chap. VI.

12. R.D. Laing describes this deadly consciousness in his *The Divided Self* (Baltimore: Pelican, 1965), pp. 106ff. Jung uses the startling image of the overbright sun, so glaring it obscures, the *sol niger,* to describe this destructive kind of consciousness. See C.G. Jung, *Mysterium Coniunctionis, CW* 14, pp. 95, 98, 145, 181, 247, 512 (pars. 113, 117, 172, 229–232, 729).

13. See Masud R. Khan, "Reparation to the Idolized Self," and "Fetish as Negation of the Self: Clinical Notes on Foreskin Fetishism in a Male Homosexual," in *Alienation in Perversions* (New York: International Universities Press, 1979); see also Khan, "The Finding and Becoming of Self," *The Privacy of the Self* (New York: International Universities Press, 1974), pp. 298–299, 301, 303.

14. See Barry Ulanov, "The Limits of Permissiveness," in *Men and Women,* ed. Philip Turner (Cambridge: Cowley, 1989).

15. For a discussion of fear of the female, see A.B. Ulanov, *Receiving Woman,* pp. 80–89, and David Holbrook, "Contempt for Woman is Contempt for Being Human," in his *The Masks of Hate* (Oxford: Pergamon Press, 1972).

16. For a discussion of the dread of the good, see A. and B. Ulanov, *Cinderella and Her Sisters,* chap. 10.

17. For an amusing example, but one which also shows the potential danger of strong fantasy, see Winnicott, *Human Nature,* p. 90: when the small boy Winnicott was treating was coming into the treatment room, he warned, "I am God!" Winnicott writes: "I knew therefore that I was to expect to be used as a bad person who ought to be punished. The intensity of the feeling was tremendous. . . . In spite of the special care I was taking I found myself hit between the eyes with a stick that he had secreted. . . . interpretation had to be made quickly before secondary considerations arose such as the idea that he ought to feel sorry for hurting me." See also Alan Edwards, "Fantasy and

Early Phases of Self-Representation," *Journal of Analytical Psychology*, 17, 1, 1972; see also R.T. MacDonald and J.A.B. Allan, "The Use of Fantasy Enactment in the Treatment of an Emerging Autistic Child," *Journal of Analytical Psychology*, 20, 1, 1975.

18. A. and B. Ulanov, *The Witch and the Clown*, chap. II.

19. A. and B. Ulanov, *Cinderella and Her Sisters*, chap. 2.

20. Gregers Werle's preaching is a bitterly ironic organ-point throughout *The Wild Duck;* Hilde Wangel's comes in streaks of rhetoric that quickly infect Solness, "the master builder," and show how powerful such identification can be. Appropriately, Hilde's intoning of the title words are the last in the play.

21. "What century am I in, what continent? Am I a child or an old man, a man or a woman, a god or a devil? Who are *you* or are you me?" asks The Stranger near the end of Part II of *To Damascus.* These words spun out to a full-length statement are emblematic of the species. See *The Plays of Strindberg*, trans. Michael Myer (New York: Vintage, 1976), II, p. 168.

22. "My life, my youth, my happiness . . . good-bye!" says Liubov Andreyevna, bidding farewell to her "beautiful orchard" at the end of Chekhov's last play. Reality has long since departed.

23. Pirandello's people do not all embrace their fantasies as cunningly and, one might almost say, as wisely as his Henry IV does. O'Neill's people, especially the figures drawn so fully from his own family in his brilliant last plays, never do so at all, never really see themselves acting out their fantasies; thus their journeys—always long, always from troubled day into the murkiest of nights.

24. See Samuel Beckett, *Krapp's Last Tape* (New York: Grove Press, 1960), p. 28.

25. There is so much adroitly made black comedy in *Rhinoceros*, one almost forgets the anti-totalitarian point of the drama, as the director and producers of the first New York performance of the play seemed to do.

26. See Tom Stoppard, *Jumpers* (New York: Grove Press,

1972), pp. 38, 71, 87, and *Travesties* (New York: Grove Press, 1975), pp. 39–40, 65, 98–99.

27. See Winnicott, *Human Nature*, pp. 116–117, 135, 137.
28. *Ibid.*, p. 80.
29. See Winnicott, *Human Nature*, p. 121.

Chapter 4: Imagination and Ministry

1. For further discussion, see A.B. Ulanov, "Picturing God," in *Picturing God*.
2. See A.B. Ulanov, "Vocation: Denying the Denial," *Anglican Theological Review*, LXXI: 2, 1989.
3. Scripture says it succinctly: "For John came neither eating nor drinking, and they say, He hath a devil. The Son of Man came eating and drinking, and they say, Behold a man gluttonous, and a winebibber, a friend of publicans and sinners" (Matthew 11:18–19).
4. See Elizabeth A. Petroff, *Medieval Women's Visionary Literature* (New York: Oxford University Press, 1986), especially p. 49.
5. For a discussion of how our personal life influences our images for God, see Ana-Marie Rizzuto, *The Hands of the Living God* (Chicago: University of Chicago Press, 1979).
6. For a discussion of subjective and objective objects, see Winnicott, *Playing and Reality*, pp. 38–39, 52, 71, 80, 100, 130.
7. For a discussion of this dream, see A.B. Ulanov, *Picturing God*, p. 174.
8. For a dream indicating our collective need for the feminine, see A.B. Ulanov, *The Feminine in Jungian Psychology and in Christian Theology* (Evanston: Northwestern University Press, 1971), pp. 271–272.
9. A further word must be said on this point. On the one hand, the objective-object God is agreed upon by countless people. They find in this god-image both enough room for and contrast to their own god-images. This *consensus gentium* God corrects private madnesses; it is precisely this agreement of the

many that the psychotic lacks. Revelation is a significant part of the objective-object God: a mysterious power grasps countless persons and converts them into believers. On the other hand, however, an objective-object god-image sanctioned by tradition, and so much used it can seem worn out and far distant from the revelatory power, can come to be used as another private god-image by specific groups, usually the ones in power. At that point, what was once thought to be universally true seems to have become a tool of manipulation for the few.

10. One of the special achievements of compact-disc technology is to have captured the richness of the French organ composers of the last hundred years. All these musicians and their best interpreters are now easily accessible to us. We can have some of the quality of the after-mass organ recital in our homes.

11. D.W. Winnicott, *Holding and Interpretation: Fragment of an Analysis* (New York: Grove Press, 1986), p. 1.

12. For a discussion of the subjective and objective layers of the text, see A.B. Ulanov, "From Image to Imago: Jung and the Study of Religion," in *Jung and the Study of Religion,* eds. L.H. Martin and James Goss (Washington: University Press of America, 1986).

13. In psychological jargon, this sharp separation of good and bad is called "splitting." See Melanie Klein, "Note on Some Schizoid Mechanisms," in *Envy and Gratitude and Other Works 1946–1963.*

14. All the sets of Paganini variations are in print on records; Blacher's *Thirteen Ways* is not, but the old Deutsche Grammophon recording does occasionally turn up in LP bins (Ernst Haefliger, with the Drolc Quartet), something worth hunting for.

Chapter 5: The People Who People Our Imagination

1. Jung says, "Sexuality is of the greatest importance as the expression of the chthonic spirit. That spirit is the 'other face of God, . . .' " C.G. Jung, *Memories, Dreams, Reflections,* p. 168.

2. See Louise Labé, *Sonnets,* trans. G.D. Martin (Austin: University of Texas Press, 1972), p. 39, and Ausias March, *Selected Poems,* trans. Arthur Tenny (Austin: University of Texas Press, 1976), pp. 91, 99, 123.

3. See *Love Story of the Dark Lord: Jayadeva's Gitagovinda,* trans. Barbara Stoller Miller (New York: Columbia University Press, 1977).

4. See Masud Khan, *Alienation in Perversions,* chaps. 5 and 6.

5. For discussion of undischarged excitement and unlived life, see A. and B. Ulanov, *The Witch and the Clown,* chap. VI.

6. Christine Downing, "Gender Anxiety," *Journal of Pastoral Care,* vol. XLIII, No. 2, Summer 1989.

7. Winnicott, *Human Nature,* p. 48.

8. Alice Miller, *Prisoners of Childhood,* trans. Ruth Ward (New York: Basic Books, 1981), p. 100. See also A.B. Ulanov, "A Shared Space: Jung and Others," in *Quadrant* (New York, C.G. Jung Foundation, 1985), pp. 74–75.

9. Winnicott, *Human Nature,* p. 45.

10. See Melanie Klein, *The Psycho-Analysis of Children,* trans. Alix Strachey (New York: Delacorte, 1975), chaps. 8 and 11. See Winnicott, *Human Nature,* p. 189 and "On the Split-off Male and Female Elements To Be Found in Men and Women," in his *Psychoanalytic Explorations,* pp. 168–183.

11. The church ought to forge the way here, we would suggest, by limiting its non-liturgical meetings to one night a week. The family life of clergy, let alone their personal life, suffers greatly from meetings three and four times a week, and indeed sometimes every day and night.

12. See C.G. Jung, *Aion: Researches into the Phenomenology of the Self,* trans. R.F.C. Hull, (New York: Pantheon, 1959), *CW* 9:2, pp. 11–23 (pars. 20–42); see also *Alchemical Studies, CW* 13, pp. 38–43 (pars. 57–63).

13. "A woman can never possess an actual penis, nor a man a vagina or a containing space. It follows that the envied object remains a part of the spiritual world, the inner world to relate to, not to possess or to be possessed. And, in the relationship, in the area of the space between objects, it is shared; not yours, or

mine but ours." B.K. Fowles, *The Journal of Analytical Psychology,* vol. 23, No. 2, April, 1978.

14. See A.B. Ulanov, "The Two Sexes," in *Men and Women,* ed. Philip Turner.

15. Jung describes the self as "one's own individual being"; ". . . the hypothetical point between conscious and unconscious"; it "epitomizes: the wholeness of the personality," in Jung, *Alchemical Studies, CW* 13, pp. 24, 45, 240 (pars. 7, 287, 36).

16. Winnicott, *Human Nature,* p. 77.

17. Winnicott, "Living Creatively" in *Home Is Where We Start From,* p. 48; see also, *ibid.*, p. 189, "This Feminism," where Winnicott writes, ". . . *to fully appreciate being a woman one has to be a man, and to fully appreciate being a man one has to be a woman.*"

18. Freud, *Totem and Taboo,* trans. James Strachey (London: Hogarth, 1953), vol. XIII of *The Standard Edition of the Complete Psychological Works of Sigmund Freud,* pp. 140–146.

19. See G.W.F. Hegel, *The Phenomenology of Mind,* trans. J.B. Baillie (New York: Macmillan, 1961), pp. 220, 225–227, 235, 247, 259. Juan Ramón Jiménez's *God Desired and Desiring* is available in a bi-lingual edition, the English translation by Antonio T. de Nicolás (New York: Paragon House, 1987), on which our translations are somewhat based. See pp. 2–3, 6–9, 12–17, 28–29, 60–64, 66–67, 76–77, 84–85, 108–109, 120–123, 126–137.

Chapter 6: Who Feeds the Feeder?

1. For a witty discussion of the helper's problem in being "larger than life," see Leslie H. Farber, "Schizophrenia and the Mad Psychotherapist," in *Lying, Despair, Jealousy, Envy, Sex, Suicide, Drugs, and the Good Life* (New York: Basic Books, 1976), pp. 104–105.

2. Harold Searles writes about this problem for the psychiatrist in "The 'Dedicated Physician' in the Field of Psychother-

apy and Psychoanalysis," in *Countertransference and Related Subjects* (New York: International Universities Press, 1979).

3. See C.G. Jung, *The Visions Seminars* (Zurich: Spring, 1976), I, p. 30.

4. "Consuming fire" is an image Paul Tillich used to refer to God. See A.B. Ulanov, "Between Anxiety and Faith: The Role of the Feminine in Tillich's Theological Thought," in *Paul Tillich on Creativity*, ed. J.A.K. Kegley (New York: University Press of America, 1989).

5. C.G. Jung, "The Stages of Life," in *The Structure and Dynamics of the Psyche*, trans. R.F.C. Hull (New York: Pantheon, 1960), *CW* 8, p. 394 (par. 771).

6. See A.B. Ulanov, "Picturing God," in *Picturing God.*

7. See C.G. Jung, "The Practical Use of Dream-Analysis" in *The Practice of Psychotherapy*, trans. R.F.C. Hull (New York: Pantheon, 1954), *CW* 16, p. 142 (par. 304).

8. The peony flower bears the transcendent to its viewer in the following scene taken from Robertson Davies' *What's Bred in the Bone* (New York: Viking, 1985), p. 62:

"It was in a garden that Francis Cornish first became truly aware of himself as a creature observing a world apart from himself. He was almost three years old, and he was looking deep into a splendid peony. He was greatly alive to himself . . . and the peony, in its fashion, was also greatly alive to itself, and the two looked at each other from their very different egotisms with solemn self-confidence. The little boy nodded at the peony and the peony seemed to nod back. The little boy was neat, clean, and pretty. The peony was unchaste, dishevelled as peonies must be, and at the height of its beauty. It was a significant moment, for it was Francis' first conspicuous encounter with beauty. . . . Every hour is filled with such moments, but with significance for someone."

9. Told to the authors by Dr. Leslie Farber, who had the story from the analyst herself.

10. The line from the early fathers, through the Middle Ages to the Renaissance and the modern world, is unbroken if one follows what might be called Augustinian principle, moving

from sign and symbol to thing and to spirit, using all the aids to be found in Augustine, Gregory the Great, Gregory of Nyssa, Bernard of Clairvaux, Thomas Aquinas, Hooker, Calvin, Pascal, John of the Cross, Luther and the like. Nicholas of Cusa offers wise words to this understanding, speaking of faith as he has earlier of intellect in his *De Docta Ignorantia:* "And if the faith of man does not attain the degree of another's because equality is impossible—just as a thing seen is not seen as exactly the same by several different people—this nevertheless is essential, that each one believe to the full power of belief that is in him." See *Of Learned Ignorance,* trans. Germain Heron (New Haven: Yale University Press, 1954), p. 163.

11. See Letter 6 of Hadewijch in *Medieval Netherlands Religious Literature,* trans. Edmund Colledge (London: Heinemann, 1965), pp. 44–45.

12. See Richard of St. Victor, *Benjamin Minor,* in *Selected Writings on Contemplation,* trans. Clare Kirchberger (New York: Harper, n.d.), pp. 91–92.

13. See Andrei Sinyavsky (writing as Abram Tertz), *Goodnight!* trans. Richard Lourie (New York: Viking, 1989), pp. 274–275, 301.

Chapter 7: Prayer and Politics

1. For a discussion of the feminine mode of being, see A.B. Ulanov, *The Feminine,* chaps. 8 and 9.

2. Karl Menninger, *The Vital Balance,* pp. 406–409.

3. See chap. 4, note 9 for concrete suggestions.

4. Thomas Merton, *Spiritual Direction and Meditation and What is Contemplation?* (Wheathamstead: Anthony Clarke, 1975), p. 46.

5. Simone Weil, *Waiting for God,* trans. Emma Crauford (New York: Capricorn, 1951), pp. 110–111.

6. Caroline Walker Bynum, "The Complexity of Symbols," in *Gender and Religion: On the Complexity of Symbols,* ed. C.W. Bynum, S. Harrell, P. Richman (Boston: Beacon, 1986), pp. 13ff.

7. Lewis Hyde, *The Gift, Imagination and the Erotic Life of*

Property (New York: Vintage of Random House, 1983), chap. 8. See also the major source of Hyde's and all related theory, Marcel Mauss, *The Gift: The Form and Reason for Exchange in Archaic Societies,* in a fine new translation by W.D. Halls with an introduction of like quality by Mary Douglas (London: Routledge, 1990).

8. See A. and B. Ulanov, *Primary Speech,* p. 20.

9. The reference is to Matisse's Chapel of the Rosary, in Vence, France, where every detail of the interior and exterior design follows a kind of painter's libretto.

10. See Wallace Stevens, *Opus Posthumous,* ed. M.J. Bates (New York: Knopf, 1989), pp. 135–138, 191, 193.

11. *Black, Brown and Beige* is available in 1944–46 and 1958 versions (Bluebird and Columbia records); "Something Sexual" is in Vol. 7 of Ellington's "Private Collection" (Saja records). The central religious statement of Duke Ellington is his Second Sacred Concert of 1968 (Prestige records).

12. An Italian Renaissance text says it very well: "Further, imagination enters into alliance with all the superior powers, inasmuch as they would fail in that function which nature has bestowed upon each of them unless imagination support and assist them. Nor could the soul, fettered as it is to the body, opine, know, or comprehend at all, if phantasy were not constantly to supply it with the images themselves." See Gianfrancesco Pico della Mirandola, *On the Imagination,* trans. Harry Caplan (New Haven: Yale University Press, 1930), p. 33.

13. The squalors of the Lysenko imagination, enforced by Stalin and others, are dramatically portrayed in *Acquired Traits: Memoirs of a Geneticist from the Soviet Union,* trans. David Lowe (New York: Viking, 1988), by Raissa L. Berg, a woman of abundant imagination and, it must be added, of heroic virtue.

14. See Vaclav Havel's first speech as President of Czechoslovakia, "The Art of the Impossible," in *The Spectator* of London, January 27, 1990, p. 11.

15. For further discussion of the feminine mode of being, see A.B. Ulanov, *Receiving Woman,* chap. 3; see also Winnicott, *Playing and Reality,* chap. 5; see also Melanie Klein, *The Psychoanalysis of Children,* chaps. 7 and 8; see also Harry Guntrip,

Schizoid Phenomena, Object Relations and the Self (New York: International Universities Press, 1969), pp. 251–264.

16. For further discussion, see A.B. Ulanov, "The Two Sexes," in *Men and Women,* ed. Philip Turner.

17. A horrendous example is the case in New York City where a young female jogger was beaten, raped, and left for dead by a group of teenagers. See Michael Stone, "What Really Happened in Central Park," in *New York Magazine,* August 14, 1989.

18. See Lois Barclay Murphy, "Play and Development," in *Play and Development,* ed. M.W. Piers.

19. Bruno Bettelheim, "Violence: A Neglected Mode of Behavior," in *Surviving and Other Essays* (New York: Knopf, 1979), p. 192.

20. See Bettelheim, "Mental Health and Urban Design," in *ibid.*

21. See Harry A. Wilner, "Vietnam and Madness: Dreams of Schizophrenic Veterans," *Journal of the American Academy of Psychoanalysis,* 10, 1, 1982; Harry Wilmer, "The Healing Nightmare: A Study of War Dreams of Vietnam Combat Veterans," *Quadrant,* 19, 1986; Harry Wilmer, "Combat Nightmares, Toward a Therapy of Violence," *Spring,* 1986.

22. See Etty Hillesum, *An Interrupted Life: The Diaries of Etty Hillesum,* trans. Arno Pomerans (New York: Pantheon, 1983); see also Etty Hillesum, *Letters From Westerbork,* trans. A.J. Pomerans (New York: Pantheon, 1986).

23. C.G. Jung, "On the Nature of the Psyche," in *The Structure and Dynamics of the Psyche,* trans. R.F.C. Hull (New York: Pantheon, 1960), *CW* 8, p. 222 (par. 428); see also Jung, *Symbols of Transformation, CW* 5, pp. 4–5, 172, 176–177 (pars. 1, 3, 252, 258–259).

24. Hillesum, *An Interrupted Life,* pp. 8, 133.

25. *Ibid.,* p. 151.

26. See Marion Milner, *On Not Being Able to Paint,* p. 140.

27. Masud Khan, "The Use and Abuse of Dream in Psychic Experience," in *The Privacy of the Self,* p. 314; see also Jung, *Symbols of Transformation, CW* 5, p. 61 (par. 95).

28. See Winnicott, "On Freedom," in *Home Is Where We Start From,* p. 237.

29. See Urs von Balthasar, *Prayer,* trans. A.V. Littledale (New York: Sheed and Ward, 1961), p. 73.

30. See Milner, *On Not Being Able to Paint,* p. 153.

31. See, for example, Otto Kernberg, *Borderline Conditions and Pathological Narcissism* (New York: Jason Aronson, 1975); see also Jules Masterson, *The Narcissistic and Borderline Disorders* (New York: Brunner Mazel, 1981); see also *Borderline Personality Disorders,* ed. Peter Hartocollis (New York: International Universities Press, 1977); Nathan Schwartz-Salant, *The Borderline Personality* (Wilmette: Chiron, 1989).

32. See A.B. Ulanov, "Vocation: Denying the Denial," *Anglican Theological Review.*

Chapter 8: Resurrection

1. Winnicott says about the interweaving of fantasy and reality, "I absolutely believe in objectivity and in looking at things straight and doing things about them; but not in making it boring by forgetting the fantasy, the unconscious fantasy." See "The Pill and the Moon," in *Home Is Where We Start From,* p. 205.

2. Jung cites the theologian Karl Rahner: "Whoever does not love the mystery, does not know God; he continuously looks past Him, the proper and true God, and worships not Him but the image of Him made to our specifications." *Schriften* VIII, p. 505, quoted in Aniela Jaffé, *Was C.G. Jung a Mystic?* trans. Diana Dachlerand, Fiona Cairns (Einsiedeln: Daimon Verlag, 1989); see also Jung, *Letters,* II, (October 1, 1953).

3. See Julian of Norwich, *The Revelations of Divine Love,* chaps. 61–62.

4. For an example and discussion of the sharp specificity of religious experience, see Pascal, *Pensées,* especially the entries on Disproportion, Imagination, and Against Indifference ("Let them at least learn what this religion is which they are attacking before attacking it.") The Penguin and Everyman editions offer

good English translations. See also "Pascal: Fire and Fact," in Barry Ulanov, *Sources and Resources: The Literary Traditions of Christian Humanism* (Westminster: Newman Press, 1960), and S.L. Frank, *God With Us,* trans. Natalie Duddington (New Haven: Yale University Press, 1946). In a required class in the Program in Psychiatry and Religion at Union Theological Seminary, taught by Ann Ulanov, one assignment asks students to cite a religious experience. Without exception, the descriptions have always emphasized concrete times, places, persons, images, events.

5. For a discussion of this point in relation to the Christian community, see H.R. Niebuhr, *The Meaning of Revelation* (New York: Macmillan, 1960), chap. 3.

6. Wittgenstein asks us to understand religious language as offering us a direct indication of what it discusses. He sees no use for religious language as referring to an unseen deity; that perpetuates a kind of pernicious dualism for him. See Fergus Kerr, *Theology After Wittgenstein* (Oxford: Blackwell, 1986), chaps. 2, 7.

7. The locus classicus for this reading is Shelley's "Ozymandias": "Look on my works, ye Mighty, and despair!"

8. See Pascal *Pensées,* trans. H.F. Stewart (New York: Pantheon, 1950), p. 115 (nos. 218, 220). The argument is an ancient one, proposed by St. Augustine and eloquently restated by Gregory the Great in the *Magna Moralia,* VI, xv, 18.

9. We will then have substituted Nietzsche's gospel for Matthew's, or reduced religion to a "God is Dead" cover story in a news magazine. How unimaginative!

10. For a discussion of this crucial aspect of Christianity, see Ann Belford Ulanov, "The God You Touch," in *The Christ and the Bodhisattva,* eds. D. Lopez and S. Rockefeller.

11. See C.G. Jung, "Psychology and Religion" in *Psychology and Religion West and East,* trans. R.F.C. Hull (New York: Pantheon, 1958), *CW* 11, p. 90 (par. 149).

12. Jung, *Psychology and Alchemy, CW* 12, pp. 265–267 (pars. 394, 396):

"The *imaginatio,* or the act of imagining, is thus a physical activity that can be fitted into the cycle of material changes that brings these about and is brought about by them in turn. In this way, the alchemist related himself not only to the unconscious but directly to the very substance which he hoped to transform through the power of the imagination. . . . Imagination is therefore a concentrated extract of the life forces, both physical and psychic . . . there did exist an intermediate realm between mind and matter, i.e., a psychic realm of subtle bodies whose characteristic is to manifest themselves in a mental as well as a material form."

"The concept *imaginatio* is perhaps the most important key to understanding of the [alchemical] *opus*. The author of the treatise "De Sulphure" speaks of the imaginative faculty of the soul. . . . The soul, he says, is the vice-regent of God. . . . The soul . . . imagines many things of the utmost profundity . . . outside the body, just as God does. But what the soul imagines happens only in the mind . . . but what God imagines happens in reality."

13. See Winnicott, *Playing and Reality*, chap. 1.

14. Jung, *Mysterium Coniunctionis*, *CW* 14, pp. 534–535 (pars. 760–763); see also p. 187 (par. 238).

15. See Schwartz-Salant, *The Borderline Personality*, pp. 7, 9, 11, 131–135.

16. See quotation in chap. I, p. 4.

17. Jung, *Psychology and Alchemy*, *CW* 12, p. 267 (par. 394).

18. See St. Augustine, *Confessions*, Book IV, chaps. 10–11.

19. See Sermon on Psalm 26(27) in *Nine Sermons of Saint Augustine on the Psalms*, trans. Edmund Hill, O.P. (London: Longmans, Green, 1958), pp. 88–89.

20. See Jaffé, *Was C.G. Jung a Mystic?* p. 110.

21. For a discussion of this idea of corresponding with grace, see A. and B. Ulanov, *Cinderella and Her Sisters*, chap. 13.

22. For a discussion of symbolic equation, see A.B. Ulanov, "Picturing God," in *Picturing God*.

23. See Elizabeth Petroff, *Medieval Women's Visionary Literature* (New York: Oxford University Press, 1986), especially the pages devoted to Catherine of Siena; see also *The Complete Works of Teresa of Avila*, trans. E. Allison Peers (New York: Sheed and Ward, 1957), II, pp. 201ff., 265, 330–331, 336; see

also Blessed John Ruysbroek, "The Book of the Sparkling Stone," in *Medieval Netherlands Religious Literature*, trans. Edmund Colledge (London: Heinemann, 1965), p. 95; see also Jacob Boehme, *The Way to Christ*, trans. Peter Erb (New York: Paulist Press, 1978), pp. 6, 10.

24. See A.B. Ulanov, "Picturing God," in *Picturing God*, p. 174.

25. Broch's *Death of Virgil* was designed as a novel, but it reads like an epic poem and deserves the meditative imagination we bring to the *Aeneid* or the *Iliad*. Musil's magnum opus, though unfinished, has a similar breadth and deserves an equal care in the reading, not out of duty, but for delight.

26. This is what Jung so often lamented and made the underlying theme of *Modern Man in Search of a Soul*, a book broken apart into separate pieces in the *Collected Works* but worth searching out in its paperback reprint integrity (Harvest books).

27. See Constance Fitzgerald, O.C.D., "Impasse and Dark Night," in *Women's Spirituality: Resources in Christian Development*, ed. J.W. Conn (Mahwah: Paulist Press, 1986).

28. See "Burnt Norton," the first of T.S. Eliot's *Four Quartets*, in *The Complete Poems and Plays 1909–1950* (New York: Harcourt, Brace, 1952), p. 120.

29. Eliot finds modern English cadences for John of the Cross in "East Coker," the second of the *Quartets*; see *ibid.*, pp. 126–127.

30. See Dietrich Bonhoeffer, *Letters and Papers from Prison*, trans. R.H. Fuller (New York: Macmillan, 1962), pp. 243–244.

31. See chap. 8, note 12.

32. This imagining was also discussed in A.B. Ulanov, "The God You Touch," pp. 131–132.

33. Etty Hillesum hit upon this reversal in the Nazi deportation camp. See Etty Hillesum, *An Interrupted Life*, pp. 36, 151, 184–185. What Hillesum discovered is at the center of the philosophical theology of Nicolas Berdyaev: In God, "opposites are naturally identified. . . . God longs for His other Self, for the free response to His love," not out of "any insufficiency," but because of "the superabundance of His plenitude and perfection." See Berdyaev, *Freedom and the Spirit* (London: Geoffrey

Bles, 1935), p. 191. A similar position is to be found in Jung, who says, "One must be able to suffer God. . . . God needs man in order to become conscious, just as he needs limitation in time and space. Let us therefore be for him limitation in time and space, an earthly tabernacle." *Letters*, I, pp. 65–66 (April 30, 1929).

34. This is the point of the eucharistic prayer about our receiving God in Christ, asking "that he may dwell in us and we in him."

35. See Thomas Merton, *Ascent of Truth* (New York: Harcourt, Brace, 1951), p. 278.

36. See Paul Ricoeur, *Freud and Philosophy: An Essay on Interpretation*, trans. Dennis Savage (New Haven: Yale University Press, 1970), p. 530.

37. See 2 Corinthians 5:21—and savor the rhetorical strength of the older translations, which do justice to the Greek and its astonishing content as few modern ones do.

38. The autobiography of St. Paul, brought to such a moving conclusion at the end of chapter two of the Letter to the Galatians, puts us all on the cross and offers rebirth from that vantage-point, where the imagination's healing strength achieves its apogee, the highest hope drawn from the most desolate moment in human history.